COMPUTE
a
DESIGN

FRACTIONS

Patricia Wright

JACOBS PUBLISHING COMPANY, INC.
PHOENIX   ARIZONA

AUTHOR Patricia Wright

Patricia Wright is presently teaching at Thirkill Elementary School in Soda Springs, Idaho. She formerly taught at Dixon Junior High School in Provo, Utah. She is also the author of the popular book **SEARCH n SHADE.** She has applied the "search n shade" concept to this new book **COMPUTE a DESIGN: Fractions** in order to provide a comprehensive review and practice program for students needing remediation in the fundamental operations with fractions.

COVER DESIGN   Robert E. Haberer

Robert E. Haberer is an art teacher at Camelback High School in Phoenix, Arizona. He was formerly the Director of Instructional Materials for the Phoenix Union High School District.

Printed in the United States of America

ISBN 0-918272-14-9

TABLE OF CONTENTS

1 FRACTIONS

Name _____

$\frac{4}{6}$	$\frac{5}{8}$	$\frac{2}{4}$	$\frac{5}{6}$	$\frac{6}{12}$	$\frac{3}{4}$	$\frac{2}{4}$	$\frac{1}{6}$	$\frac{7}{8}$	$\frac{5}{8}$
$\frac{7}{8}$	$\frac{1}{3}$	$\frac{3}{10}$	$\frac{4}{5}$	$\frac{3}{8}$	$\frac{1}{3}$	$\frac{1}{4}$	$\frac{2}{6}$	$\frac{3}{8}$	$\frac{4}{6}$
$\frac{2}{5}$	$\frac{3}{4}$	$\frac{1}{3}$	$\frac{1}{6}$	$\frac{2}{6}$	$\frac{3}{4}$	$\frac{2}{4}$	$\frac{3}{8}$	$\frac{4}{5}$	$\frac{5}{6}$
$\frac{4}{5}$	$\frac{7}{9}$	$\frac{3}{8}$	$\frac{2}{5}$	$\frac{7}{9}$	$\frac{7}{9}$	$\frac{1}{6}$	$\frac{1}{3}$	$\frac{7}{9}$	$\frac{3}{10}$
$\frac{5}{6}$	$\frac{2}{6}$	$\frac{7}{9}$	$\frac{3}{10}$	$\frac{5}{8}$	$\frac{7}{8}$	$\frac{6}{12}$	$\frac{7}{9}$	$\frac{3}{4}$	$\frac{2}{5}$
$\frac{1}{4}$	$\frac{2}{5}$	$\frac{3}{4}$	$\frac{2}{5}$	$\frac{1}{6}$	$\frac{1}{3}$	$\frac{1}{6}$	$\frac{4}{5}$	$\frac{3}{8}$	$\frac{4}{5}$
$\frac{1}{3}$	$\frac{7}{9}$	$\frac{7}{9}$	$\frac{5}{6}$	$\frac{2}{4}$	$\frac{3}{8}$	$\frac{1}{3}$	$\frac{7}{9}$	$\frac{7}{9}$	$\frac{5}{6}$
$\frac{7}{9}$	$\frac{3}{4}$	$\frac{4}{5}$	$\frac{7}{9}$	$\frac{3}{10}$	$\frac{2}{6}$	$\frac{7}{9}$	$\frac{1}{4}$	$\frac{6}{12}$	$\frac{7}{9}$
$\frac{6}{12}$	$\frac{1}{6}$	$\frac{4}{6}$	$\frac{7}{8}$	$\frac{2}{4}$	$\frac{3}{8}$	$\frac{5}{8}$	$\frac{7}{8}$	$\frac{1}{3}$	$\frac{3}{4}$
$\frac{5}{8}$	$\frac{2}{6}$	$\frac{7}{9}$	$\frac{7}{9}$	$\frac{3}{8}$	$\frac{2}{5}$	$\frac{7}{9}$	$\frac{7}{9}$	$\frac{1}{4}$	$\frac{4}{6}$

Write a fraction to show what part of each figure is shaded.

 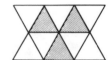

    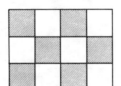   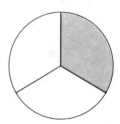

   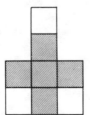 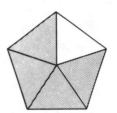

 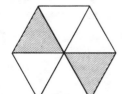  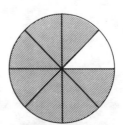 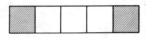

$\frac{7}{8}$	$\frac{3}{4}$	$\frac{2}{7}$	$\frac{3}{8}$	$\frac{7}{12}$	$\frac{7}{4}$	$\frac{1}{2}$	$\frac{4}{3}$	$\frac{3}{4}$	$\frac{1}{6}$
$\frac{10}{12}$	$\frac{3}{5}$	$\frac{5}{7}$	$\frac{5}{2}$	$\frac{3}{8}$	$\frac{1}{2}$	$\frac{7}{16}$	$\frac{7}{8}$	$\frac{1}{6}$	$\frac{10}{12}$
$\frac{6}{10}$	$\frac{5}{2}$	$\frac{5}{9}$	$\frac{3}{5}$	$\frac{7}{4}$	$\frac{5}{6}$	$\frac{3}{8}$	$\frac{5}{6}$	$\frac{5}{9}$	$\frac{6}{10}$
$\frac{5}{2}$	$\frac{1}{6}$	$\frac{7}{8}$	$\frac{7}{16}$	$\frac{1}{2}$	$\frac{5}{7}$	$\frac{7}{12}$	$\frac{5}{7}$	$\frac{3}{5}$	$\frac{7}{4}$
$\frac{3}{8}$	$\frac{5}{6}$	$\frac{7}{16}$	$\frac{3}{5}$	$\frac{5}{9}$	$\frac{7}{12}$	$\frac{5}{7}$	$\frac{7}{12}$	$\frac{7}{4}$	$\frac{7}{8}$
$\frac{5}{9}$	$\frac{1}{2}$	$\frac{1}{6}$	$\frac{5}{2}$	$\frac{1}{6}$	$\frac{3}{5}$	$\frac{7}{16}$	$\frac{7}{8}$	$\frac{3}{8}$	$\frac{5}{6}$
$\frac{1}{2}$	$\frac{7}{16}$	$\frac{5}{2}$	$\frac{5}{7}$	$\frac{5}{6}$	$\frac{5}{9}$	$\frac{3}{5}$	$\frac{7}{4}$	$\frac{7}{12}$	$\frac{1}{6}$
$\frac{7}{14}$	$\frac{1}{2}$	$\frac{3}{8}$	$\frac{7}{12}$	$\frac{5}{7}$	$\frac{7}{8}$	$\frac{7}{4}$	$\frac{3}{5}$	$\frac{1}{6}$	$\frac{7}{14}$
$\frac{15}{27}$	$\frac{5}{2}$	$\frac{7}{16}$	$\frac{1}{2}$	$\frac{5}{9}$	$\frac{5}{6}$	$\frac{3}{8}$	$\frac{7}{12}$	$\frac{7}{4}$	$\frac{15}{27}$
$\frac{5}{2}$	$\frac{4}{3}$	$\frac{2}{7}$	$\frac{7}{16}$	$\frac{7}{8}$	$\frac{5}{7}$	$\frac{5}{6}$	$\frac{3}{4}$	$\frac{2}{7}$	$\frac{5}{9}$

Reduce to lowest terms.

 $\frac{6}{8}$

 $\frac{9}{24}$

$\frac{15}{6}$

$\frac{21}{36}$ $\frac{14}{8}$ $\frac{21}{24}$ $\frac{15}{21}$

$\frac{20}{24}$ $\frac{8}{6}$ $\frac{30}{54}$ $\frac{14}{28}$

$\frac{21}{48}$ $\frac{12}{20}$ $\frac{10}{35}$ $\frac{5}{30}$

3 IMPROPER FRACTIONS

$3\frac{3}{4}$	$6\frac{1}{2}$	$2\frac{1}{4}$	$1\frac{5}{6}$	$7\frac{1}{3}$	$3\frac{5}{9}$	$5\frac{7}{8}$	$6\frac{1}{2}$	$2\frac{1}{4}$	$3\frac{3}{4}$
$2\frac{1}{4}$	$3\frac{3}{4}$	$3\frac{5}{9}$	$2\frac{3}{8}$	$6\frac{2}{3}$	$5\frac{1}{4}$	$6\frac{3}{4}$	$6\frac{5}{7}$	$2\frac{1}{4}$	$6\frac{1}{2}$
$6\frac{1}{2}$	$7\frac{2}{9}$	$8\frac{3}{7}$	$2\frac{1}{4}$	$3\frac{3}{4}$	$6\frac{1}{2}$	$2\frac{1}{4}$	$3\frac{1}{7}$	$7\frac{1}{3}$	$3\frac{3}{4}$
$2\frac{1}{4}$	$6\frac{3}{4}$	$6\frac{2}{3}$	$1\frac{5}{6}$	$2\frac{3}{8}$	$6\frac{3}{4}$	$7\frac{1}{3}$	$3\frac{1}{7}$	$8\frac{3}{7}$	$2\frac{1}{4}$
$3\frac{3}{4}$	$6\frac{1}{2}$	$2\frac{1}{4}$	$5\frac{1}{4}$	$6\frac{5}{7}$	$7\frac{2}{9}$	$8\frac{3}{7}$	$6\frac{1}{2}$	$2\frac{1}{4}$	$6\frac{1}{2}$
$3\frac{5}{9}$	$5\frac{7}{8}$	$3\frac{3}{4}$	$6\frac{1}{2}$	$3\frac{3}{4}$	$2\frac{1}{4}$	$6\frac{1}{2}$	$3\frac{3}{4}$	$7\frac{2}{9}$	$7\frac{1}{3}$
$6\frac{2}{3}$	$5\frac{1}{4}$	$7\frac{1}{3}$	$1\frac{5}{6}$	$8\frac{1}{9}$	$8\frac{1}{9}$	$5\frac{7}{8}$	$3\frac{5}{9}$	$2\frac{3}{8}$	$5\frac{1}{4}$
$2\frac{1}{4}$	$6\frac{1}{2}$	$6\frac{3}{4}$	$2\frac{3}{8}$	$3\frac{5}{9}$	$6\frac{5}{7}$	$3\frac{1}{7}$	$8\frac{3}{7}$	$2\frac{1}{4}$	$6\frac{1}{2}$
$6\frac{1}{2}$	$3\frac{3}{4}$	$1\frac{5}{6}$	$6\frac{5}{7}$	$6\frac{3}{4}$	$6\frac{2}{3}$	$1\frac{5}{6}$	$5\frac{7}{8}$	$3\frac{3}{4}$	$2\frac{1}{4}$
$2\frac{1}{4}$	$7\frac{2}{9}$	$2\frac{3}{8}$	$3\frac{1}{7}$	$8\frac{1}{9}$	$8\frac{1}{9}$	$8\frac{3}{7}$	$5\frac{1}{4}$	$7\frac{1}{3}$	$6\frac{1}{2}$

Change to mixed numbers.

■ $\dfrac{15}{4}$

◩ $\dfrac{11}{6}$

◪ $\dfrac{20}{3}$

◪ $\dfrac{19}{8}$ ◨ $\dfrac{22}{7}$ ◱ $\dfrac{22}{3}$ ◪ $\dfrac{32}{9}$

◪ $\dfrac{59}{7}$ ■ $\dfrac{13}{2}$ ◩ $\dfrac{27}{4}$ ◱ $\dfrac{47}{7}$

◩ $\dfrac{21}{4}$ � $\dfrac{47}{8}$ ■ $\dfrac{9}{4}$ ◪ $\dfrac{65}{9}$

4 IMPROPER FRACTIONS Name _____

$2\frac{8}{10}$	$2\frac{2}{5}$	$8\frac{1}{2}$	$2\frac{2}{5}$	$3\frac{1}{3}$	$1\frac{3}{4}$	$3\frac{3}{8}$	$4\frac{1}{2}$	$3\frac{5}{6}$	$2\frac{8}{10}$
$2\frac{1}{3}$	$3\frac{1}{4}$	$2\frac{4}{7}$	$3\frac{3}{5}$	$1\frac{7}{8}$	$3\frac{5}{6}$	$2\frac{1}{2}$	$3\frac{3}{8}$	$1\frac{3}{4}$	$2\frac{1}{2}$
$1\frac{7}{8}$	$3\frac{3}{5}$	$2\frac{12}{14}$	$1\frac{7}{8}$	$3\frac{1}{4}$	$3\frac{1}{3}$	$2\frac{4}{5}$	$2\frac{12}{14}$	$1\frac{1}{4}$	$3\frac{5}{6}$
$8\frac{1}{2}$	$2\frac{4}{7}$	$8\frac{1}{2}$	$1\frac{3}{4}$	$2\frac{2}{5}$	$3\frac{5}{6}$	$3\frac{1}{3}$	$2\frac{1}{2}$	$2\frac{4}{5}$	$2\frac{1}{2}$
$3\frac{1}{3}$	$2\frac{1}{3}$	$3\frac{1}{4}$	$3\frac{3}{5}$	$3\frac{1}{3}$	$3\frac{1}{4}$	$4\frac{1}{2}$	$3\frac{1}{3}$	$1\frac{1}{4}$	$3\frac{1}{4}$
$3\frac{1}{4}$	$2\frac{4}{5}$	$1\frac{3}{4}$	$3\frac{3}{8}$	$1\frac{3}{4}$	$3\frac{1}{3}$	$1\frac{7}{8}$	$1\frac{3}{4}$	$2\frac{4}{7}$	$3\frac{1}{3}$
$3\frac{5}{6}$	$1\frac{1}{4}$	$2\frac{4}{5}$	$3\frac{1}{4}$	$4\frac{1}{2}$	$2\frac{1}{3}$	$3\frac{1}{4}$	$2\frac{2}{5}$	$3\frac{3}{5}$	$1\frac{7}{8}$
$2\frac{1}{2}$	$3\frac{5}{6}$	$1\frac{12}{16}$	$2\frac{1}{2}$	$3\frac{1}{3}$	$1\frac{3}{4}$	$8\frac{1}{2}$	$1\frac{12}{16}$	$1\frac{7}{8}$	$8\frac{1}{2}$
$3\frac{3}{8}$	$3\frac{1}{3}$	$1\frac{1}{4}$	$3\frac{3}{8}$	$2\frac{1}{2}$	$3\frac{3}{5}$	$2\frac{2}{5}$	$3\frac{3}{5}$	$1\frac{3}{4}$	$2\frac{4}{7}$
$3\frac{6}{8}$	$2\frac{1}{2}$	$3\frac{5}{6}$	$4\frac{1}{2}$	$3\frac{1}{4}$	$3\frac{1}{3}$	$8\frac{1}{2}$	$2\frac{4}{7}$	$2\frac{1}{3}$	$3\frac{6}{8}$

Change to mixed numbers. Reduce.

■ $\frac{26}{8}$

◩ $\frac{18}{4}$

◩ $\frac{54}{16}$

◩ $\frac{46}{12}$ ◩ $\frac{24}{10}$ ◪ $\frac{21}{9}$ ◩ $\frac{15}{6}$

◩ $\frac{56}{20}$ ■ $\frac{30}{9}$ ◣ $\frac{30}{16}$ ◸ $\frac{51}{6}$

◣ $\frac{36}{14}$ ◺ $\frac{36}{10}$ ■ $\frac{14}{8}$ ◩ $\frac{15}{12}$

5 DECIMALS

$\frac{3}{5}$	$3\frac{37}{100}$	$\frac{3}{20}$	$2\frac{1}{2}$	$2\frac{7}{10}$	$\frac{3}{20}$	$1\frac{1}{4}$	$1\frac{4}{5}$	$\frac{3}{250}$	$2\frac{1}{2}$
$\frac{31}{100}$	$1\frac{1}{4}$	$\frac{3}{25}$	$3\frac{2}{5}$	$\frac{3}{5}$	$2\frac{1}{2}$	$\frac{1}{2}$	$3\frac{17}{50}$	$\frac{3}{5}$	$\frac{3}{25}$
$\frac{3}{250}$	$\frac{7}{25}$	$2\frac{1}{2}$	$\frac{3}{250}$	$\frac{7}{25}$	$\frac{31}{100}$	$3\frac{37}{100}$	$1\frac{1}{4}$	$3\frac{2}{5}$	$2\frac{7}{10}$
$3\frac{17}{50}$	$3\frac{37}{100}$	$2\frac{1}{50}$	$\frac{3}{25}$	$\frac{3}{20}$	$2\frac{7}{10}$	$3\frac{2}{5}$	$2\frac{7}{10}$	$\frac{3}{20}$	$\frac{1}{2}$
$1\frac{4}{5}$	$3\frac{2}{5}$	$\frac{3}{5}$	$2\frac{7}{10}$	$\frac{3}{250}$	$1\frac{4}{5}$	$\frac{3}{250}$	$2\frac{1}{2}$	$\frac{7}{25}$	$\frac{3}{20}$
$2\frac{1}{2}$	$2\frac{7}{10}$	$\frac{31}{100}$	$1\frac{1}{4}$	$\frac{7}{25}$	$3\frac{17}{50}$	$1\frac{1}{4}$	$\frac{3}{25}$	$\frac{3}{250}$	$\frac{3}{5}$
$\frac{3}{5}$	$\frac{1}{2}$	$2\frac{1}{50}$	$\frac{1}{2}$	$\frac{3}{20}$	$1\frac{4}{5}$	$3\frac{2}{5}$	$2\frac{7}{10}$	$3\frac{17}{50}$	$2\frac{1}{2}$
$\frac{7}{25}$	$\frac{3}{250}$	$2\frac{1}{2}$	$3\frac{37}{100}$	$\frac{31}{100}$	$\frac{3}{25}$	$2\frac{1}{50}$	$2\frac{1}{2}$	$1\frac{4}{5}$	$3\frac{2}{5}$
$\frac{3}{20}$	$\frac{3}{5}$	$1\frac{1}{4}$	$\frac{3}{5}$	$1\frac{4}{5}$	$\frac{3}{250}$	$\frac{3}{5}$	$1\frac{1}{4}$	$2\frac{1}{2}$	$3\frac{37}{100}$
$3\frac{2}{5}$	$2\frac{1}{2}$	$\frac{3}{25}$	$\frac{31}{100}$	$2\frac{1}{2}$	$1\frac{1}{4}$	$\frac{7}{25}$	$\frac{31}{100}$	$\frac{3}{5}$	$\frac{1}{2}$

Change to a fraction or mixed number. Reduce if possible.

■ .6

◩ .12

◪ .15

◩ .012   ◫ 3.37   ◨ 3.4   ◩ .28

◩ 2.020   ■ 2.5   ◣ 1.80   ◨ .31

◣ 2.7   ◧ 3.34   ◤ 1.25   ◩ .5

6 MIXED NUMBERS

Name _____

Change to fractions.
Reduce if possible.

$\frac{13}{6}$	$\frac{27}{8}$	$\frac{17}{6}$	$\frac{35}{16}$	$\frac{12}{5}$	$\frac{11}{4}$	$\frac{12}{7}$	$\frac{10}{3}$	$\frac{19}{10}$	$\frac{17}{7}$
$\frac{11}{4}$	$\frac{13}{4}$	$\frac{35}{16}$	$\frac{19}{8}$	$\frac{7}{4}$	$\frac{13}{4}$	$\frac{8}{5}$	$\frac{12}{7}$	$\frac{7}{4}$	$\frac{19}{10}$
$\frac{17}{6}$	$\frac{27}{8}$	$\frac{19}{8}$	$\frac{11}{4}$	$\frac{12}{5}$	$\frac{35}{16}$	$\frac{19}{10}$	$\frac{8}{5}$	$\frac{12}{5}$	$\frac{10}{3}$
$\frac{27}{8}$	$\frac{17}{6}$	$\frac{11}{4}$	$\frac{13}{4}$	$\frac{7}{4}$	$\frac{19}{8}$	$\frac{8}{5}$	$\frac{12}{7}$	$\frac{10}{3}$	$\frac{19}{10}$
$\frac{7}{4}$	$\frac{12}{5}$	$\frac{8}{5}$	$\frac{12}{5}$	$\frac{23}{4}$	$\frac{13}{6}$	$\frac{35}{16}$	$\frac{17}{6}$	$\frac{27}{8}$	$\frac{19}{8}$
$\frac{11}{4}$	$\frac{13}{4}$	$\frac{35}{16}$	$\frac{19}{8}$	$\frac{17}{7}$	$\frac{23}{4}$	$\frac{10}{3}$	$\frac{19}{10}$	$\frac{8}{5}$	$\frac{12}{5}$
$\frac{7}{4}$	$\frac{19}{10}$	$\frac{10}{3}$	$\frac{12}{7}$	$\frac{11}{4}$	$\frac{12}{5}$	$\frac{27}{8}$	$\frac{17}{6}$	$\frac{35}{16}$	$\frac{13}{4}$
$\frac{19}{10}$	$\frac{7}{4}$	$\frac{12}{7}$	$\frac{10}{3}$	$\frac{19}{8}$	$\frac{8}{5}$	$\frac{17}{6}$	$\frac{27}{8}$	$\frac{13}{4}$	$\frac{35}{16}$
$\frac{7}{4}$	$\frac{12}{5}$	$\frac{10}{3}$	$\frac{19}{10}$	$\frac{11}{4}$	$\frac{12}{7}$	$\frac{27}{8}$	$\frac{13}{4}$	$\frac{35}{16}$	$\frac{19}{8}$
$\frac{17}{7}$	$\frac{8}{5}$	$\frac{12}{7}$	$\frac{10}{3}$	$\frac{17}{6}$	$\frac{7}{4}$	$\frac{13}{4}$	$\frac{27}{8}$	$\frac{19}{8}$	$\frac{23}{4}$

■ $5\frac{3}{4}$

◪ $2\frac{6}{8}$

◪ $2\frac{5}{6}$

◩ $3\frac{1}{4}$ ◩ $3\frac{2}{6}$ � $2\frac{4}{10}$ ◪ $3\frac{3}{8}$

◪ $2\frac{6}{16}$ ■ $2\frac{2}{12}$ ◣ $1\frac{3}{5}$ ◹ $1\frac{9}{10}$

◣ $1\frac{12}{16}$ ◪ $1\frac{10}{14}$ ■ $2\frac{3}{7}$ ◪ $2\frac{3}{16}$

Name _____

$\frac{6}{7}$	$\frac{17}{20}$	$\frac{9}{16}$	$2\frac{1}{3}$	$1\frac{1}{8}$	$\frac{5}{8}$	$\frac{8}{9}$	1	$\frac{9}{11}$	$1\frac{1}{3}$
$\frac{8}{9}$	$\frac{5}{8}$	$1\frac{1}{7}$	$1\frac{2}{5}$	$\frac{9}{11}$	$\frac{3}{4}$	$\frac{5}{8}$	$1\frac{1}{7}$	$1\frac{1}{3}$	$\frac{5}{7}$
$\frac{1}{2}$	$\frac{3}{4}$	$\frac{8}{9}$	$\frac{17}{20}$	1	$\frac{9}{16}$	$\frac{5}{7}$	$\frac{5}{7}$	$\frac{9}{11}$	$\frac{1}{2}$
$\frac{9}{16}$	1	$\frac{1}{2}$	$\frac{7}{15}$	$1\frac{1}{8}$	$\frac{6}{7}$	$1\frac{1}{3}$	$\frac{9}{16}$	1	$\frac{9}{16}$
$\frac{6}{7}$	$\frac{5}{8}$	$\frac{6}{7}$	$\frac{8}{9}$	$1\frac{2}{11}$	$1\frac{1}{7}$	$2\frac{1}{3}$	$1\frac{2}{5}$	$1\frac{1}{8}$	$1\frac{2}{5}$
$1\frac{2}{11}$	$1\frac{1}{7}$	$\frac{3}{4}$	$\frac{1}{2}$	$\frac{5}{7}$	$\frac{3}{4}$	$\frac{9}{16}$	$\frac{9}{11}$	$1\frac{2}{11}$	$1\frac{1}{7}$
$2\frac{1}{3}$	$\frac{9}{11}$	1	$\frac{6}{7}$	$\frac{9}{16}$	$\frac{1}{2}$	$1\frac{2}{5}$	1	$\frac{17}{20}$	$\frac{8}{9}$
$\frac{1}{2}$	$\frac{9}{16}$	$\frac{5}{8}$	$1\frac{2}{11}$	$1\frac{2}{5}$	$\frac{7}{15}$	$1\frac{2}{11}$	$1\frac{1}{8}$	$\frac{1}{2}$	$\frac{9}{16}$
$1\frac{1}{3}$	$1\frac{1}{8}$	$1\frac{1}{7}$	$\frac{8}{9}$	$1\frac{2}{11}$	$1\frac{1}{7}$	$\frac{9}{11}$	$1\frac{1}{7}$	$\frac{7}{15}$	$\frac{5}{8}$
$1\frac{1}{7}$	$1\frac{2}{11}$	$\frac{17}{20}$	1	$\frac{5}{7}$	$\frac{17}{20}$	$\frac{1}{2}$	$2\frac{1}{3}$	$1\frac{2}{11}$	$1\frac{1}{7}$

Reduce each answer if possible.

■ $\frac{5}{16}$ $+ \frac{4}{16}$

◩ $\frac{5}{15} + \frac{2}{15}$

◩ $\frac{5}{9}$ $+ \frac{3}{9}$

◩ $\frac{3}{8}$ $+ \frac{3}{8}$

◤ $\frac{3}{7} + \frac{2}{7}$

◸ $\frac{4}{5}$ $+ \frac{3}{5}$

◩ $\frac{5}{7} + \frac{1}{7}$

◤ $\frac{8}{20}$ $+ \frac{9}{20}$

■ $\frac{13}{15} + \frac{2}{15}$

◥ $\frac{5}{6}$ $+ \frac{9}{6}$

◸ $\frac{7}{8}$ $+ \frac{2}{8}$

◥ $\frac{4}{11}$ $+ \frac{5}{11}$

◸ $\frac{8}{9} + \frac{4}{9}$

■ $\frac{3}{8}$ $+ \frac{1}{8}$

◩ $\frac{1}{8} + \frac{4}{8}$

8 ADDITION

$9\frac{6}{9}$	$4\frac{7}{9}$	$7\frac{2}{8}$	$8\frac{4}{10}$	$7\frac{3}{4}$	$6\frac{3}{4}$	$8\frac{4}{10}$	$7\frac{2}{8}$	$8\frac{2}{5}$	$9\frac{6}{9}$
$7\frac{1}{2}$	$8\frac{2}{5}$	$7\frac{1}{2}$	$6\frac{6}{16}$	$3\frac{8}{16}$	$3\frac{8}{16}$	$6\frac{6}{16}$	$7\frac{1}{2}$	$4\frac{7}{9}$	$8\frac{2}{5}$
$6\frac{6}{8}$	$4\frac{7}{9}$	$7\frac{6}{13}$	$9\frac{2}{3}$	$3\frac{1}{2}$	$3\frac{5}{8}$	$7\frac{4}{5}$	$7\frac{6}{13}$	$4\frac{7}{9}$	$6\frac{6}{8}$
$3\frac{10}{16}$	$7\frac{6}{14}$	$8\frac{4}{5}$	$7\frac{6}{7}$	$6\frac{8}{9}$	$5\frac{1}{2}$	$6\frac{6}{13}$	$7\frac{1}{4}$	$7\frac{6}{14}$	$3\frac{10}{16}$
$7\frac{4}{5}$	$7\frac{4}{16}$	$7\frac{3}{4}$	$3\frac{1}{2}$	$3\frac{5}{8}$	$7\frac{1}{4}$	$8\frac{4}{5}$	$6\frac{3}{4}$	$7\frac{4}{16}$	$9\frac{2}{3}$
$5\frac{1}{2}$	$7\frac{4}{16}$	$3\frac{5}{8}$	$7\frac{6}{7}$	$6\frac{6}{13}$	$5\frac{1}{2}$	$6\frac{8}{9}$	$7\frac{4}{5}$	$7\frac{4}{16}$	$7\frac{3}{4}$
$3\frac{10}{16}$	$7\frac{6}{14}$	$6\frac{8}{9}$	$7\frac{4}{5}$	$3\frac{5}{8}$	$3\frac{1}{2}$	$9\frac{2}{3}$	$6\frac{3}{4}$	$7\frac{6}{14}$	$3\frac{10}{16}$
$6\frac{6}{8}$	$7\frac{1}{2}$	$7\frac{6}{13}$	$7\frac{3}{4}$	$7\frac{6}{7}$	$6\frac{6}{13}$	$5\frac{1}{2}$	$7\frac{6}{13}$	$4\frac{7}{9}$	$6\frac{6}{8}$
$8\frac{2}{5}$	$4\frac{7}{9}$	$8\frac{2}{5}$	$6\frac{6}{16}$	$3\frac{8}{16}$	$3\frac{8}{16}$	$6\frac{6}{16}$	$7\frac{1}{2}$	$8\frac{2}{5}$	$7\frac{1}{2}$
$9\frac{6}{9}$	$4\frac{7}{9}$	$7\frac{2}{8}$	$8\frac{4}{10}$	$8\frac{4}{5}$	$7\frac{1}{4}$	$8\frac{4}{10}$	$7\frac{2}{8}$	$7\frac{1}{2}$	$9\frac{6}{9}$

Reduce each answer if possible.

■ $5\frac{3}{8}$
    $+\,2\frac{1}{8}$

◨ $6\frac{4}{7}$
    $+\,1\frac{2}{7}$

◪ $3\frac{7}{16}$
    $+\ \ \frac{3}{16}$

◥ $4\frac{2}{9}$
  $+\,5\frac{4}{9}$

◤ $2\frac{3}{16}$
  $+\,1\frac{5}{16}$

◺ $4\frac{1}{9}$
  $+\,2\frac{7}{9}$

◥ $2\frac{5}{8}$
  $+\,4\frac{1}{8}$

◸ $4\frac{2}{5}$
  $+\,4\frac{2}{5}$

■ $3\frac{2}{9}$
  $+\,1\frac{5}{9}$

◨ $3\frac{1}{8}$
  $+\,4\frac{1}{8}$

◩ 4
  $+\,3\frac{3}{4}$

� ◺ $3\frac{1}{5}$
  $+\,4\frac{3}{5}$

◩ $6\frac{1}{13}$
  $+\ \ \frac{5}{13}$

■ $6\frac{1}{10}$
  $+\,2\frac{3}{10}$

◥ $5\frac{1}{12}$
  $+\ \ \frac{5}{12}$

9 ADDITION

Name ______________________

$8\frac{1}{5}$	$8\frac{3}{11}$	$10\frac{3}{10}$	$10\frac{5}{6}$	$13\frac{1}{8}$	$5\frac{5}{12}$	$9\frac{5}{9}$	$18\frac{1}{10}$	$5\frac{3}{5}$	$8\frac{1}{5}$
$16\frac{1}{12}$	$10\frac{1}{8}$	$7\frac{4}{7}$	$5\frac{3}{5}$	$6\frac{3}{7}$	$9\frac{4}{11}$	$6\frac{3}{7}$	$13\frac{1}{8}$	$6\frac{2}{9}$	$10\frac{5}{6}$
$9\frac{4}{11}$	$5\frac{5}{12}$	$10\frac{3}{10}$	$7\frac{4}{7}$	$16\frac{1}{12}$	$7\frac{4}{7}$	$13\frac{1}{8}$	$18\frac{1}{10}$	$16\frac{1}{12}$	$8\frac{3}{11}$
$10\frac{5}{6}$	$9\frac{4}{11}$	$9\frac{3}{5}$	$18\frac{1}{10}$	$10\frac{3}{10}$	$6\frac{3}{7}$	$10\frac{3}{10}$	$6\frac{2}{9}$	$8\frac{3}{11}$	$9\frac{5}{9}$
$8\frac{3}{11}$	$9\frac{5}{9}$	$6\frac{2}{9}$	$10\frac{1}{8}$	$9\frac{3}{5}$	$6\frac{2}{9}$	$10\frac{1}{8}$	$9\frac{3}{5}$	$5\frac{5}{12}$	$10\frac{3}{10}$
$5\frac{5}{12}$	$5\frac{3}{5}$	$10\frac{5}{6}$	$6\frac{2}{9}$	$7\frac{4}{7}$	$13\frac{1}{8}$	$9\frac{3}{5}$	$16\frac{1}{12}$	$6\frac{3}{7}$	$16\frac{1}{12}$
$18\frac{1}{10}$	$16\frac{1}{12}$	$18\frac{1}{10}$	$9\frac{5}{9}$	$8\frac{1}{5}$	$8\frac{1}{5}$	$7\frac{4}{7}$	$9\frac{4}{11}$	$5\frac{5}{12}$	$9\frac{4}{11}$
$9\frac{5}{9}$	$6\frac{3}{7}$	$13\frac{1}{8}$	$6\frac{3}{7}$	$5\frac{3}{5}$	$8\frac{3}{11}$	$5\frac{3}{5}$	$7\frac{4}{7}$	$5\frac{3}{5}$	$10\frac{5}{6}$
$10\frac{3}{10}$	$10\frac{1}{8}$	$8\frac{3}{11}$	$9\frac{5}{9}$	$7\frac{4}{7}$	$13\frac{1}{8}$	$10\frac{5}{6}$	$9\frac{4}{11}$	$6\frac{2}{9}$	$18\frac{1}{10}$
$8\frac{1}{5}$	$5\frac{5}{12}$	$13\frac{1}{8}$	$18\frac{1}{10}$	$9\frac{4}{11}$	$18\frac{1}{10}$	$10\frac{3}{10}$	$7\frac{4}{7}$	$16\frac{1}{12}$	$8\frac{1}{5}$

■ $6\frac{4}{5} + 2\frac{4}{5}$

◤ $1\frac{5}{12} + 3\frac{12}{12}$

◢ $5\frac{8}{10} + 4\frac{5}{10}$

◢ $\frac{10}{11} + 8\frac{5}{11}$

◣ $\frac{5}{7} + 5\frac{5}{7}$

◥ $4\frac{7}{9} + 4\frac{7}{9}$

◤ $5\frac{3}{7} + 1\frac{8}{7}$

◢ $4\frac{4}{5} + \frac{4}{5}$

■ $4\frac{7}{9} + 1\frac{4}{9}$

◣ $\frac{7}{11} + 7\frac{7}{11}$

◥ $3\frac{2}{8} + 9\frac{7}{8}$

◣ $8\frac{7}{10} + 9\frac{4}{10}$

◥ $8\frac{7}{12} + 7\frac{6}{12}$

■ $6\frac{5}{8} + 3\frac{4}{8}$

◤ $2\frac{3}{6} + 7\frac{8}{6}$

Name _____

$1\frac{6}{7}$	$1\frac{7}{8}$	$4\frac{3}{7}$	$2\frac{2}{11}$	$1\frac{3}{4}$	$1\frac{6}{7}$	$2\frac{2}{11}$	$3\frac{5}{12}$	$6\frac{9}{10}$	$1\frac{3}{4}$
$2\frac{2}{15}$	$10\frac{1}{8}$	$2\frac{2}{15}$	$6\frac{9}{10}$	$1\frac{6}{7}$	$2\frac{2}{11}$	$1\frac{7}{8}$	$4\frac{5}{6}$	$9\frac{1}{7}$	$2\frac{5}{14}$
$9\frac{1}{7}$	$2\frac{5}{14}$	$12\frac{8}{11}$	$8\frac{3}{16}$	$4\frac{7}{8}$	$2\frac{5}{14}$	$9\frac{1}{7}$	$4\frac{3}{7}$	$2\frac{2}{15}$	$10\frac{1}{8}$
$1\frac{3}{4}$	$5\frac{5}{6}$	$4\frac{5}{6}$	$1\frac{7}{8}$	$4\frac{3}{7}$	$9\frac{1}{7}$	$6\frac{9}{10}$	$4\frac{7}{8}$	$5\frac{5}{6}$	$1\frac{3}{4}$
$1\frac{7}{8}$	$10\frac{1}{8}$	$3\frac{5}{12}$	$8\frac{3}{16}$	$4\frac{7}{8}$	$2\frac{5}{14}$	$3\frac{5}{12}$	$8\frac{3}{16}$	$3\frac{5}{12}$	$2\frac{5}{14}$
$4\frac{3}{7}$	$1\frac{3}{4}$	$1\frac{6}{7}$	$2\frac{2}{11}$	$1\frac{3}{4}$	$1\frac{6}{7}$	$2\frac{2}{11}$	$1\frac{3}{4}$	$1\frac{6}{7}$	$12\frac{8}{11}$
$6\frac{9}{10}$	$2\frac{2}{11}$	$1\frac{3}{4}$	$4\frac{7}{8}$	$5\frac{5}{6}$	$5\frac{5}{6}$	$4\frac{5}{6}$	$1\frac{6}{7}$	$2\frac{2}{11}$	$2\frac{2}{15}$
$3\frac{5}{12}$	$4\frac{5}{6}$	$1\frac{6}{7}$	$5\frac{5}{6}$	$2\frac{2}{11}$	$1\frac{6}{7}$	$5\frac{5}{6}$	$1\frac{3}{4}$	$4\frac{7}{8}$	$8\frac{3}{16}$
$1\frac{6}{7}$	$12\frac{8}{11}$	$2\frac{5}{14}$	$3\frac{5}{12}$	$5\frac{5}{6}$	$5\frac{5}{6}$	$10\frac{1}{8}$	$1\frac{7}{8}$	$10\frac{1}{8}$	$1\frac{3}{4}$
$2\frac{2}{11}$	$1\frac{3}{4}$	$9\frac{1}{7}$	$6\frac{9}{10}$	$2\frac{2}{11}$	$1\frac{3}{4}$	$2\frac{2}{15}$	$4\frac{3}{7}$	$2\frac{2}{11}$	$1\frac{6}{7}$

■ $\frac{3}{7} + \frac{4}{7} + \frac{6}{7}$

◨ $\frac{5}{8} + \frac{7}{8} + \frac{3}{8}$

◪ $1\frac{5}{7} + 2\frac{2}{7} + \frac{3}{7}$

◪ $3\frac{1}{8} + 2\frac{5}{8} + 4\frac{3}{8}$ ◤ $2\frac{1}{12} + \frac{9}{12} + \frac{7}{12}$ ◹ $\frac{9}{14} + \frac{11}{14} + \frac{13}{14}$ ◸ $\frac{11}{15} + \frac{7}{15} + \frac{14}{15}$

◩ $\frac{9}{16} + 5\frac{3}{16} + 2\frac{7}{16}$ ■ $\frac{8}{11} + \frac{9}{11} + \frac{7}{11}$ ◣ $5\frac{5}{11} + \frac{8}{11} + 6\frac{6}{11}$ ◥ $5\frac{7}{10} + \frac{3}{10} + \frac{9}{10}$

◣ $\frac{6}{7} + 4\frac{5}{7} + 3\frac{4}{7}$ ◨ $2\frac{1}{6} + \frac{5}{6} + 1\frac{5}{6}$ ■ $\frac{3}{4} + \frac{1}{4} + \frac{3}{4}$ ◹ $2\frac{5}{8} + \frac{7}{8} + 1\frac{3}{8}$

11 ADDITION

$2\frac{1}{4}$	$4\frac{1}{2}$	$8\frac{1}{2}$	$10\frac{1}{3}$	15	$6\frac{1}{4}$	$20\frac{1}{5}$	$8\frac{1}{2}$	15	$4\frac{1}{4}$
$4\frac{2}{3}$	$3\frac{1}{3}$	$6\frac{1}{4}$	5	$2\frac{2}{3}$	$7\frac{1}{5}$	$4\frac{1}{2}$	$2\frac{1}{4}$	$4\frac{2}{3}$	$7\frac{1}{5}$
$4\frac{1}{4}$	$10\frac{1}{3}$	$18\frac{1}{4}$	12	$20\frac{1}{5}$	$8\frac{1}{2}$	$3\frac{1}{3}$	12	$10\frac{1}{3}$	5
$18\frac{1}{4}$	$6\frac{1}{4}$	$8\frac{1}{2}$	$2\frac{1}{4}$	$10\frac{1}{3}$	$20\frac{1}{5}$	$6\frac{1}{4}$	$8\frac{1}{2}$	15	$2\frac{2}{3}$
15	12	5	$4\frac{2}{3}$	$2\frac{1}{4}$	$4\frac{1}{4}$	$7\frac{1}{5}$	$4\frac{1}{2}$	$18\frac{1}{4}$	$6\frac{1}{4}$
$3\frac{1}{3}$	$4\frac{1}{2}$	$8\frac{1}{2}$	$10\frac{1}{3}$	$7\frac{1}{5}$	12	$20\frac{1}{5}$	$8\frac{1}{2}$	$2\frac{1}{4}$	12
$20\frac{1}{5}$	$7\frac{1}{5}$	$6\frac{1}{4}$	$18\frac{1}{4}$	$4\frac{1}{4}$	5	$2\frac{2}{3}$	5	$4\frac{2}{3}$	$10\frac{1}{3}$
$8\frac{1}{2}$	5	$2\frac{2}{3}$	$20\frac{1}{5}$	$3\frac{1}{3}$	12	$10\frac{1}{3}$	$3\frac{1}{3}$	$6\frac{1}{4}$	$20\frac{1}{5}$
$2\frac{1}{4}$	12	$10\frac{1}{3}$	15	$4\frac{1}{2}$	5	$4\frac{1}{2}$	$8\frac{1}{2}$	$7\frac{1}{5}$	$4\frac{1}{2}$
$3\frac{1}{3}$	$4\frac{1}{4}$	$2\frac{1}{4}$	$4\frac{2}{3}$	$7\frac{1}{5}$	$4\frac{2}{3}$	$18\frac{1}{4}$	$6\frac{1}{4}$	15	12

Reduce each answer if possible.

■ $7\frac{1}{4} + \frac{2}{4} + \frac{3}{4}$

◩ $5\frac{4}{5} + \frac{3}{5} + 8\frac{3}{5}$

◣ $1\frac{1}{3} + 1\frac{2}{3} + 1\frac{2}{3}$

◢ $\frac{8}{9} + \frac{8}{9} + \frac{8}{9}$

◥ $2\frac{12}{15} + \frac{4}{15} + 4\frac{2}{15}$

◤ $2\frac{15}{16} + \frac{3}{16} + 3\frac{2}{16}$

◥ $\frac{6}{7} + 3\frac{4}{7} + \frac{4}{7}$

◣ $3\frac{5}{11} + \frac{10}{11} + 7\frac{7}{11}$

■ $2\frac{8}{6} + 2\frac{2}{6} + 4\frac{4}{6}$

◣ $2\frac{4}{6} + \frac{1}{6} + \frac{3}{6}$

◤ $2\frac{5}{12} + \frac{7}{12} + 1\frac{3}{12}$

◣ $6\frac{4}{8} + 8\frac{1}{8} + 3\frac{5}{8}$

◤ $1\frac{5}{8} + 2\frac{4}{8} + \frac{3}{8}$

■ $5\frac{8}{10} + 4\frac{5}{10} + 9\frac{9}{10}$

◥ $\frac{5}{8} + \frac{7}{8} + \frac{6}{8}$

Name _____

$6\frac{2}{3}$	$4\frac{7}{8}$	$8\frac{1}{2}$	$1\frac{1}{2}$	$7\frac{1}{5}$	$13\frac{3}{5}$	$4\frac{7}{8}$	$3\frac{1}{4}$	$8\frac{2}{7}$	$1\frac{1}{2}$
$4\frac{7}{8}$	$6\frac{2}{3}$	$\frac{11}{13}$	$1\frac{1}{9}$	$3\frac{1}{4}$	$8\frac{1}{2}$	$1\frac{1}{8}$	$\frac{12}{17}$	$1\frac{1}{2}$	$3\frac{1}{4}$
$8\frac{1}{2}$	$\frac{11}{13}$	$\frac{12}{17}$	$\frac{2}{3}$	$5\frac{1}{3}$	$8\frac{2}{5}$	$\frac{2}{3}$	$\frac{11}{13}$	$\frac{2}{3}$	$8\frac{2}{7}$
$5\frac{7}{11}$	$8\frac{2}{7}$	$\frac{2}{3}$	$\frac{11}{13}$	$8\frac{2}{5}$	$5\frac{1}{3}$	$\frac{11}{13}$	$\frac{12}{17}$	$6\frac{2}{3}$	$1\frac{1}{8}$
$1\frac{1}{2}$	$1\frac{1}{9}$	$5\frac{1}{3}$	$8\frac{2}{5}$	$3\frac{9}{10}$	$5\frac{7}{11}$	$5\frac{1}{3}$	$8\frac{2}{5}$	$3\frac{9}{10}$	$4\frac{7}{8}$
$7\frac{1}{5}$	$8\frac{2}{7}$	$\frac{11}{13}$	$\frac{2}{3}$	$6\frac{2}{3}$	$8\frac{2}{7}$	$\frac{12}{17}$	$\frac{2}{3}$	$8\frac{1}{2}$	$1\frac{1}{8}$
$1\frac{1}{9}$	$5\frac{7}{11}$	$1\frac{1}{9}$	$7\frac{1}{5}$	$1\frac{1}{8}$	$7\frac{1}{5}$	$3\frac{9}{10}$	$13\frac{3}{5}$	$1\frac{1}{8}$	$3\frac{9}{10}$
$5\frac{7}{11}$	$7\frac{1}{5}$	$1\frac{1}{9}$	$13\frac{3}{5}$	$\frac{12}{17}$	$\frac{11}{13}$	$1\frac{1}{9}$	$3\frac{9}{10}$	$13\frac{3}{5}$	$1\frac{1}{8}$
$1\frac{1}{9}$	$1\frac{1}{9}$	$5\frac{7}{11}$	$7\frac{1}{5}$	$3\frac{1}{4}$	$8\frac{1}{2}$	$13\frac{3}{5}$	$1\frac{1}{8}$	$3\frac{9}{10}$	$13\frac{3}{5}$
$7\frac{1}{5}$	$5\frac{7}{11}$	$1\frac{1}{9}$	$5\frac{7}{11}$	$1\frac{1}{9}$	$1\frac{1}{8}$	$3\frac{9}{10}$	$13\frac{3}{5}$	$1\frac{1}{8}$	$3\frac{9}{10}$

■ $\dfrac{9}{13} + \dfrac{2}{13}$

◨ $\begin{aligned} &4\frac{2}{9} \\ +\,&2\frac{4}{9} \end{aligned}$

◪ $3 + \dfrac{9}{10}$

◨ $\begin{aligned} &\frac{15}{16} \\ +\,&\frac{3}{16} \end{aligned}$

◨ $\begin{aligned} &4\frac{9}{15} \\ +\,&2\frac{9}{15} \end{aligned}$

◩ $\begin{aligned} &2\frac{7}{8} \\ +\,&\frac{3}{8} \end{aligned}$

◨ $\dfrac{3}{8} + 4\frac{4}{8}$

◨ $\begin{aligned} &7\frac{1}{5} \\ +\,&6\frac{2}{5} \end{aligned}$

■ $\dfrac{7}{12} + \dfrac{1}{12}$

� $\begin{aligned} &5\frac{4}{11} \\ +\,&\frac{3}{11} \end{aligned}$

� $\begin{aligned} &2\frac{3}{7} \\ +\,&5\frac{6}{7} \end{aligned}$

� $\begin{aligned} &\frac{9}{18} \\ +\,&\frac{11}{18} \end{aligned}$

◹ $\begin{aligned} &\frac{1}{4} \\ +\,&\frac{5}{4} \end{aligned}$

■ $\dfrac{9}{17} + \dfrac{3}{17}$

◨ $\begin{aligned} &4\frac{7}{8} \\ +\,&3\frac{5}{8} \end{aligned}$

13 SUBTRACTION

Name _____

$\frac{5}{12}$	$\frac{1}{9}$	$\frac{7}{11}$	$\frac{5}{12}$	$\frac{7}{11}$	$\frac{1}{9}$	$\frac{5}{12}$	$\frac{7}{11}$	$\frac{5}{12}$	$\frac{1}{9}$
$\frac{7}{11}$	$\frac{1}{3}$	$\frac{2}{3}$	$\frac{1}{5}$	$\frac{4}{5}$	$\frac{1}{3}$	$\frac{2}{3}$	$\frac{1}{2}$	$\frac{1}{4}$	$\frac{5}{12}$
$\frac{1}{9}$	$\frac{1}{5}$	$\frac{6}{7}$	$\frac{2}{5}$	$\frac{2}{3}$	$\frac{5}{8}$	$\frac{4}{5}$	$\frac{1}{3}$	$\frac{2}{3}$	$\frac{7}{11}$
$\frac{5}{12}$	$\frac{2}{5}$	$\frac{3}{8}$	$\frac{1}{2}$	$\frac{6}{7}$	$\frac{2}{5}$	$\frac{3}{8}$	$\frac{5}{8}$	$\frac{6}{7}$	$\frac{1}{9}$
$\frac{1}{9}$	$\frac{1}{2}$	$\frac{4}{5}$	$\frac{1}{3}$	$\frac{3}{8}$	$\frac{1}{2}$	$\frac{6}{7}$	$\frac{2}{5}$	$\frac{3}{8}$	$\frac{5}{12}$
$\frac{5}{12}$	$\frac{5}{7}$	$\frac{3}{7}$	$\frac{5}{8}$	$\frac{1}{4}$	$\frac{5}{7}$	$\frac{3}{7}$	$\frac{1}{5}$	$\frac{4}{5}$	$\frac{1}{9}$
$\frac{7}{11}$	$\frac{5}{8}$	$\frac{4}{5}$	$\frac{5}{7}$	$\frac{3}{7}$	$\frac{1}{5}$	$\frac{6}{7}$	$\frac{5}{7}$	$\frac{3}{7}$	$\frac{7}{11}$
$\frac{1}{9}$	$\frac{2}{5}$	$\frac{3}{8}$	$\frac{1}{2}$	$\frac{4}{5}$	$\frac{2}{5}$	$\frac{3}{8}$	$\frac{5}{8}$	$\frac{1}{4}$	$\frac{1}{9}$
$\frac{7}{11}$	$\frac{1}{2}$	$\frac{1}{4}$	$\frac{2}{5}$	$\frac{2}{3}$	$\frac{5}{8}$	$\frac{6}{7}$	$\frac{2}{5}$	$\frac{3}{8}$	$\frac{5}{12}$
$\frac{1}{9}$	$\frac{7}{11}$	$\frac{5}{12}$	$\frac{1}{9}$	$\frac{7}{11}$	$\frac{7}{11}$	$\frac{1}{9}$	$\frac{5}{12}$	$\frac{7}{11}$	$\frac{1}{9}$

Reduce each answer if possible.

■ $\frac{9}{12} - \frac{4}{12}$

◪ $\frac{15}{16} - \frac{5}{16}$

◪ $\frac{13}{14} - \frac{1}{14}$

◰ $\frac{13}{20} - \frac{8}{20}$

◳ $\frac{20}{21} - \frac{5}{21}$

◳ $\frac{5}{6} - \frac{1}{6}$

◰ $\frac{7}{8} - \frac{3}{8}$

◰ $\frac{9}{10} - \frac{1}{10}$

■ $\frac{8}{9} - \frac{7}{9}$

◪ $\frac{13}{24} - \frac{5}{24}$

◳ $\frac{19}{32} - \frac{7}{32}$

◪ $\frac{14}{15} - \frac{8}{15}$

◳ $\frac{4}{7} - \frac{1}{7}$

■ $\frac{10}{11} - \frac{3}{11}$

◰ $\frac{6}{15} - \frac{3}{15}$

14 SUBTRACTION

Name _____

$1\frac{1}{2}$	$5\frac{2}{7}$	$2\frac{3}{11}$	$8\frac{6}{17}$	$4\frac{3}{5}$	$3\frac{5}{9}$	$4\frac{1}{3}$	$4\frac{1}{4}$	$5\frac{2}{7}$	$6\frac{3}{5}$
$6\frac{3}{5}$	$4\frac{3}{5}$	$5\frac{2}{3}$	$3\frac{7}{19}$	$5\frac{1}{7}$	$4\frac{1}{2}$	$5\frac{2}{3}$	$4\frac{1}{2}$	$3\frac{5}{9}$	$1\frac{1}{2}$
$4\frac{1}{3}$	$1\frac{1}{3}$	$4\frac{3}{5}$	$1\frac{1}{2}$	$5\frac{2}{7}$	$6\frac{3}{5}$	$5\frac{2}{7}$	$4\frac{1}{4}$	$3\frac{7}{19}$	$8\frac{6}{17}$
$5\frac{1}{7}$	$2\frac{3}{11}$	$7\frac{2}{11}$	$1\frac{1}{3}$	$2\frac{3}{11}$	$8\frac{6}{17}$	$3\frac{7}{19}$	$7\frac{2}{11}$	$3\frac{5}{9}$	$7\frac{1}{4}$
$5\frac{2}{7}$	$1\frac{1}{2}$	$5\frac{1}{7}$	$4\frac{3}{5}$	$1\frac{1}{3}$	$3\frac{7}{19}$	$3\frac{5}{9}$	$4\frac{1}{2}$	$6\frac{3}{5}$	$6\frac{3}{5}$
$1\frac{1}{2}$	$4\frac{1}{4}$	$4\frac{1}{3}$	$7\frac{2}{11}$	$8\frac{1}{5}$	$7\frac{2}{11}$	$8\frac{1}{5}$	$4\frac{1}{4}$	$4\frac{1}{3}$	$1\frac{1}{2}$
$4\frac{1}{4}$	$4\frac{1}{2}$	$1\frac{1}{3}$	$8\frac{1}{5}$	$7\frac{2}{11}$	$8\frac{1}{5}$	$7\frac{2}{11}$	$7\frac{1}{4}$	$5\frac{1}{7}$	$4\frac{1}{3}$
$4\frac{1}{2}$	$3\frac{5}{9}$	$6\frac{3}{5}$	$1\frac{1}{3}$	$7\frac{1}{4}$	$5\frac{2}{3}$	$3\frac{7}{19}$	$1\frac{1}{2}$	$4\frac{3}{5}$	$5\frac{1}{7}$
$6\frac{3}{5}$	$7\frac{1}{4}$	$8\frac{6}{17}$	$4\frac{1}{3}$	$3\frac{5}{9}$	$4\frac{3}{5}$	$8\frac{6}{17}$	$2\frac{3}{11}$	$1\frac{1}{3}$	$5\frac{2}{7}$
$5\frac{2}{7}$	$6\frac{3}{5}$	$3\frac{7}{19}$	$5\frac{1}{7}$	$4\frac{1}{2}$	$1\frac{1}{3}$	$7\frac{1}{4}$	$5\frac{2}{3}$	$1\frac{1}{2}$	$6\frac{3}{5}$

Reduce each answer if possible.

$$\blacksquare \quad 8\frac{4}{5} \\ -2\frac{1}{5}$$

$$\diagup\!\!\!\square \quad 6\frac{8}{11} \\ -4\frac{5}{11}$$

$$\diagup\!\!\!\blacksquare \quad 9\frac{10}{21} \\ -4\frac{7}{21}$$

$$\diagup\!\!\!\blacksquare \quad 6\frac{5}{6} \\ -5\frac{3}{6}$$

$$\blacksquare\!\!\diagdown \quad 6\frac{18}{19} \\ -3\frac{11}{19}$$

$$\square\!\!\diagdown \quad 8\frac{11}{17} \\ -\ \ \frac{5}{17}$$

$$\diagup\!\!\!\blacksquare \quad 5\frac{21}{25} \\ -1\frac{6}{25}$$

$$\diagup\!\!\!\blacksquare \quad 8\frac{8}{9} \\ -3\frac{2}{9}$$

$$\blacksquare \quad 8\frac{6}{7} \\ -3\frac{4}{7}$$

$$\diagup\!\!\!\blacksquare \quad 8\frac{9}{16} \\ -1\frac{5}{16}$$

$$\square\!\!\diagdown \quad 8\frac{5}{9} \\ -5$$

$$\square\!\!\diagdown \quad 6\frac{9}{12} \\ -2\frac{3}{12}$$

$$\square\!\!\diagdown \quad 4\frac{5}{8} \\ -\ \ \frac{3}{8}$$

$$\blacksquare \quad 7\frac{9}{10} \\ -6\frac{4}{10}$$

$$\diagup\!\!\!\blacksquare \quad 9\frac{12}{18} \\ -5\frac{6}{18}$$

15 SUBTRACTION

Name _____

$7\frac{2}{7}$	$3\frac{1}{2}$	$4\frac{5}{7}$	$2\frac{7}{9}$	$2\frac{6}{7}$	$2\frac{7}{16}$	$4\frac{12}{13}$	$\frac{8}{15}$	$3\frac{1}{2}$	$7\frac{2}{7}$
$7\frac{2}{3}$	$2\frac{8}{11}$	$2\frac{7}{16}$	$3\frac{5}{8}$	$2\frac{8}{11}$	$4\frac{7}{9}$	$6\frac{5}{6}$	$3\frac{5}{8}$	$5\frac{4}{5}$	$7\frac{2}{3}$
$5\frac{9}{14}$	$1\frac{9}{11}$	$\frac{9}{10}$	$4\frac{5}{7}$	$\frac{8}{15}$	$4\frac{12}{13}$	$2\frac{7}{9}$	$5\frac{9}{14}$	$\frac{8}{15}$	$2\frac{6}{7}$
$1\frac{5}{12}$	$3\frac{5}{8}$	$6\frac{5}{6}$	$2\frac{7}{9}$	$6\frac{5}{6}$	$\frac{9}{10}$	$1\frac{9}{11}$	$3\frac{5}{8}$	$6\frac{5}{6}$	$4\frac{12}{13}$
$2\frac{6}{7}$	$5\frac{4}{5}$	$1\frac{5}{12}$	$4\frac{5}{7}$	$1\frac{5}{12}$	$4\frac{12}{13}$	$\frac{8}{15}$	$1\frac{9}{11}$	$4\frac{7}{9}$	$2\frac{7}{16}$
$4\frac{12}{13}$	$2\frac{8}{11}$	$6\frac{5}{6}$	$2\frac{6}{7}$	$6\frac{5}{6}$	$\frac{9}{10}$	$5\frac{9}{14}$	$3\frac{5}{8}$	$2\frac{8}{11}$	$2\frac{7}{9}$
$2\frac{7}{16}$	$4\frac{5}{7}$	$2\frac{7}{9}$	$5\frac{9}{14}$	$2\frac{7}{9}$	$4\frac{5}{7}$	$2\frac{6}{7}$	$4\frac{12}{13}$	$1\frac{5}{12}$	$2\frac{6}{7}$
$\frac{8}{15}$	$3\frac{5}{8}$	$1\frac{9}{11}$	$2\frac{6}{7}$	$5\frac{9}{14}$	$\frac{9}{10}$	$2\frac{7}{16}$	$\frac{8}{15}$	$5\frac{9}{14}$	$1\frac{9}{11}$
$3\frac{1}{2}$	$5\frac{4}{5}$	$\frac{8}{15}$	$4\frac{12}{13}$	$2\frac{8}{11}$	$4\frac{7}{9}$	$\frac{8}{15}$	$4\frac{12}{13}$	$4\frac{7}{9}$	$3\frac{1}{2}$
$7\frac{2}{7}$	$7\frac{2}{3}$	$3\frac{5}{8}$	$6\frac{5}{6}$	$4\frac{5}{7}$	$2\frac{7}{9}$	$\frac{9}{10}$	$6\frac{5}{6}$	$7\frac{2}{3}$	$7\frac{2}{7}$

■ $6\frac{1}{5}$ $-\ \frac{2}{5}$

◨ $1\frac{7}{15}$ $-\ \frac{14}{15}$

◪ $4\frac{5}{7}$ $-1\frac{6}{7}$

◪ $4\frac{3}{8}$ $-\ \frac{6}{8}$

◨ $3\frac{1}{16}$ $-\ \frac{10}{16}$

◱ $6\frac{3}{7}$ $-1\frac{5}{7}$

◪ $3\frac{5}{9}$ $-\ \frac{7}{9}$

◪ $5\frac{3}{10}$ $-4\frac{4}{10}$

■ $8\frac{6}{9}$ $-3\frac{8}{9}$

◨ $8\frac{4}{14}$ $-2\frac{9}{14}$

◳ $2\frac{5}{11}$ $-\ \frac{7}{11}$

◧ $10\frac{1}{6}$ $-\ 3\frac{2}{6}$

◰ $9\frac{6}{13}$ $-4\frac{7}{13}$

■ $7\frac{6}{11}$ $-4\frac{9}{11}$

◪ $5\frac{1}{12}$ $-3\frac{8}{12}$

Name _____

$4\frac{4}{5}$	$2\frac{4}{7}$	$8\frac{3}{4}$	$6\frac{1}{7}$	$3\frac{5}{9}$	$8\frac{4}{5}$	$6\frac{1}{7}$	$2\frac{4}{7}$	$6\frac{1}{7}$	$2\frac{1}{3}$
$8\frac{3}{4}$	$6\frac{1}{7}$	$9\frac{7}{10}$	$3\frac{5}{13}$	$8\frac{3}{4}$	$2\frac{4}{7}$	$1\frac{1}{3}$	$3\frac{5}{13}$	$8\frac{3}{4}$	$2\frac{4}{7}$
$2\frac{4}{7}$	$1\frac{3}{8}$	$8\frac{2}{7}$	$2\frac{1}{3}$	$9\frac{7}{10}$	$3\frac{5}{13}$	$8\frac{2}{7}$	$7\frac{1}{6}$	$6\frac{4}{9}$	$6\frac{1}{7}$
$6\frac{1}{7}$	$5\frac{2}{3}$	$1\frac{1}{3}$	$6\frac{4}{9}$	$7\frac{1}{6}$	$4\frac{4}{5}$	$1\frac{3}{8}$	$4\frac{11}{15}$	$5\frac{2}{3}$	$8\frac{3}{4}$
$8\frac{3}{4}$	$5\frac{2}{3}$	$8\frac{4}{5}$	$3\frac{5}{9}$	$9\frac{7}{10}$	$4\frac{11}{15}$	$2\frac{1}{3}$	$3\frac{5}{9}$	$5\frac{2}{3}$	$2\frac{4}{7}$
$2\frac{4}{7}$	$2\frac{1}{3}$	$3\frac{5}{13}$	$1\frac{3}{8}$	$8\frac{4}{5}$	$8\frac{2}{7}$	$6\frac{4}{9}$	$9\frac{7}{10}$	$3\frac{5}{9}$	$6\frac{1}{7}$
$6\frac{1}{7}$	$8\frac{3}{4}$	$6\frac{1}{7}$	$9\frac{7}{10}$	$4\frac{11}{15}$	$1\frac{3}{8}$	$3\frac{5}{13}$	$6\frac{1}{7}$	$8\frac{3}{4}$	$2\frac{4}{7}$
$8\frac{3}{4}$	$2\frac{4}{7}$	$1\frac{3}{8}$	$8\frac{2}{7}$	$7\frac{1}{6}$	$4\frac{4}{5}$	$7\frac{1}{6}$	$6\frac{4}{9}$	$8\frac{3}{4}$	$6\frac{1}{7}$
$6\frac{4}{9}$	$6\frac{1}{7}$	$2\frac{1}{3}$	$3\frac{5}{13}$	$6\frac{1}{7}$	$2\frac{4}{7}$	$1\frac{1}{3}$	$4\frac{4}{5}$	$6\frac{1}{7}$	$1\frac{1}{3}$
$5\frac{2}{3}$	$4\frac{11}{15}$	$2\frac{4}{7}$	$8\frac{4}{5}$	$5\frac{2}{3}$	$5\frac{2}{3}$	$8\frac{2}{7}$	$2\frac{4}{7}$	$1\frac{3}{8}$	$5\frac{2}{3}$

■ $\begin{array}{r} 7 \\ -\ \frac{6}{7} \\ \hline \end{array}$

◪ $\begin{array}{r} 10 \\ -\ \frac{3}{10} \\ \hline \end{array}$

◪ $8 - 4\frac{4}{9}$

◪ $\begin{array}{r} 13 \\ -\ 4\frac{5}{7} \\ \hline \end{array}$

◣ $\begin{array}{r} 9 \\ -\ \frac{1}{5} \\ \hline \end{array}$

◻ $\begin{array}{r} 5 \\ -1\frac{8}{13} \\ \hline \end{array}$

◪ $3 - 1\frac{5}{8}$

◪ $5 - \frac{1}{5}$

■ $6 - 3\frac{3}{7}$

◣ $8 - \frac{5}{6}$

◻ $\begin{array}{r} 7 \\ -\ \frac{5}{9} \\ \hline \end{array}$

◣ $\begin{array}{r} 5 \\ -2\frac{2}{3} \\ \hline \end{array}$

◪ $8 - 3\frac{4}{15}$

■ $9 - \frac{1}{4}$

◪ $\begin{array}{r} 5 \\ -3\frac{2}{3} \\ \hline \end{array}$

17 COMPARING FRACTIONS   Name _____

$\frac{5}{10}$	$\frac{7}{8}$	$\frac{4}{5}$	$\frac{5}{10}$	$\frac{7}{8}$	$\frac{4}{5}$	$\frac{7}{8}$	$\frac{4}{5}$	$\frac{5}{10}$	$\frac{7}{8}$
$\frac{4}{5}$	$\frac{5}{10}$	$\frac{9}{14}$	$\frac{3}{5}$	$\frac{4}{5}$	$\frac{5}{10}$	$\frac{3}{5}$	$\frac{4}{6}$	$\frac{4}{5}$	$\frac{4}{5}$
$\frac{7}{8}$	$\frac{8}{9}$	$\frac{4}{5}$	$\frac{9}{17}$	$\frac{6}{14}$	$\frac{9}{11}$	$\frac{4}{9}$	$\frac{7}{8}$	$\frac{11}{12}$	$\frac{5}{10}$
$\frac{5}{10}$	$\frac{9}{17}$	$\frac{3}{5}$	$\frac{4}{9}$	$\frac{9}{14}$	$\frac{17}{36}$	$\frac{9}{17}$	$\frac{3}{5}$	$\frac{4}{9}$	$\frac{7}{8}$
$\frac{5}{10}$	$\frac{7}{8}$	$\frac{11}{16}$	$\frac{6}{14}$	$\frac{7}{8}$	$\frac{4}{5}$	$\frac{6}{7}$	$\frac{3}{7}$	$\frac{5}{10}$	$\frac{4}{5}$
$\frac{7}{8}$	$\frac{5}{10}$	$\frac{9}{11}$	$\frac{3}{7}$	$\frac{4}{5}$	$\frac{5}{10}$	$\frac{4}{7}$	$\frac{7}{9}$	$\frac{7}{8}$	$\frac{4}{5}$
$\frac{4}{5}$	$\frac{4}{9}$	$\frac{9}{17}$	$\frac{3}{5}$	$\frac{6}{7}$	$\frac{7}{9}$	$\frac{4}{9}$	$\frac{3}{5}$	$\frac{9}{17}$	$\frac{5}{10}$
$\frac{5}{10}$	$\frac{4}{6}$	$\frac{4}{5}$	$\frac{4}{9}$	$\frac{3}{7}$	$\frac{11}{16}$	$\frac{9}{17}$	$\frac{4}{5}$	$\frac{11}{16}$	$\frac{7}{8}$
$\frac{4}{5}$	$\frac{7}{8}$	$\frac{11}{12}$	$\frac{3}{5}$	$\frac{4}{5}$	$\frac{5}{10}$	$\frac{3}{5}$	$\frac{8}{9}$	$\frac{5}{10}$	$\frac{4}{5}$
$\frac{7}{8}$	$\frac{5}{10}$	$\frac{4}{5}$	$\frac{7}{8}$	$\frac{5}{10}$	$\frac{7}{8}$	$\frac{5}{10}$	$\frac{4}{5}$	$\frac{7}{8}$	$\frac{7}{8}$

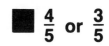

Choose the larger number.

■ $\frac{4}{5}$ or $\frac{3}{5}$

◪ $\frac{8}{11}$ or $\frac{9}{11}$

◪ $\frac{4}{6}$ or $\frac{4}{9}$

◪ $\frac{3}{7}$ or $\frac{3}{14}$ ◨ $\frac{4}{7}$ or $\frac{4}{9}$ ◧ $\frac{8}{11}$ or $\frac{8}{9}$ ◪ $\frac{7}{12}$ or $\frac{11}{12}$

◪ $\frac{17}{36}$ or $\frac{5}{36}$ ■ $\frac{4}{8}$ or $\frac{7}{8}$ ◨ $\frac{7}{16}$ or $\frac{11}{16}$ ◧ $\frac{7}{9}$ or $\frac{5}{9}$

◨ $\frac{9}{17}$ or $\frac{9}{14}$ ◧ $\frac{6}{14}$ or $\frac{6}{15}$ ■ $\frac{5}{12}$ or $\frac{5}{10}$ ◪ $\frac{6}{7}$ or $\frac{6}{9}$

Name _____

$\frac{5}{13}$	$\frac{4}{5}$	$8\frac{1}{12}$	$14\frac{3}{4}$	$3\frac{4}{5}$	$\frac{5}{13}$	$5\frac{1}{2}$	$\frac{9}{13}$	$\frac{4}{5}$	$\frac{5}{13}$
$3\frac{4}{5}$	$5\frac{1}{2}$	$1\frac{1}{3}$	$2\frac{5}{8}$	$\frac{6}{13}$	$\frac{8}{11}$	$6\frac{2}{9}$	$10\frac{1}{5}$	$3\frac{4}{7}$	$3\frac{4}{5}$
$\frac{8}{9}$	$4\frac{1}{2}$	$\frac{8}{9}$	$3\frac{4}{7}$	$3\frac{4}{5}$	$\frac{5}{13}$	$\frac{8}{9}$	$\frac{9}{13}$	$7\frac{2}{3}$	$14\frac{3}{4}$
$10\frac{1}{5}$	$\frac{9}{13}$	$\frac{4}{5}$	$\frac{6}{13}$	$\frac{4}{5}$	$3\frac{4}{5}$	$\frac{6}{13}$	$\frac{4}{5}$	$\frac{8}{9}$	$1\frac{1}{3}$
$\frac{5}{13}$	$\frac{4}{5}$	$3\frac{4}{5}$	$7\frac{2}{3}$	$3\frac{4}{7}$	$5\frac{1}{2}$	$4\frac{1}{2}$	$\frac{5}{13}$	$3\frac{4}{5}$	$\frac{5}{13}$
$3\frac{4}{5}$	$\frac{5}{13}$	$5\frac{1}{2}$	$\frac{4}{5}$	$10\frac{1}{5}$	$6\frac{2}{9}$	$\frac{4}{5}$	$3\frac{4}{7}$	$\frac{4}{5}$	$3\frac{4}{5}$
$\frac{4}{5}$	$8\frac{1}{12}$	$\frac{8}{11}$	$\frac{6}{13}$	$3\frac{4}{5}$	$\frac{5}{13}$	$\frac{6}{13}$	$\frac{8}{11}$	$14\frac{3}{4}$	$\frac{4}{5}$
$3\frac{4}{5}$	$\frac{5}{13}$	$\frac{8}{11}$	$\frac{6}{13}$	$\frac{9}{13}$	$8\frac{1}{12}$	$\frac{6}{13}$	$\frac{8}{11}$	$3\frac{4}{5}$	$\frac{5}{13}$
$\frac{5}{13}$	$\frac{4}{5}$	$3\frac{4}{5}$	$\frac{4}{5}$	$2\frac{5}{8}$	$4\frac{1}{2}$	$\frac{4}{5}$	$\frac{5}{13}$	$\frac{4}{5}$	$3\frac{4}{5}$
$3\frac{4}{5}$	$\frac{5}{13}$	$\frac{4}{5}$	$\frac{5}{13}$	$\frac{4}{5}$	$3\frac{4}{5}$	$\frac{5}{13}$	$\frac{4}{5}$	$\frac{5}{13}$	$3\frac{4}{5}$

Reduce each answer if possible.

■ $\frac{7}{13} - \frac{2}{13}$

◪ $9 - \frac{11}{12}$

◪ $5\frac{20}{21} - 4\frac{13}{21}$

◪ $5\frac{1}{4} - \frac{3}{4}$

◪ $8\frac{11}{12} - 1\frac{3}{12}$

◹ $4\frac{1}{7} - \frac{4}{7}$

◪ $7\frac{5}{8} - 2\frac{1}{8}$

◪ $9\frac{1}{9} - 2\frac{8}{9}$

■ $\frac{14}{15} - \frac{2}{15}$

◩ $5\frac{15}{16} - 3\frac{5}{16}$

◹ $14\frac{7}{8} - \frac{1}{8}$

◩ $12\frac{7}{10} - 2\frac{5}{10}$

◹ Which is larger? $\frac{6}{13}$ or $\frac{9}{13}$

■ $8 - 4\frac{1}{5}$

◹ Which is larger? $\frac{8}{9}$ or $\frac{8}{11}$

19 LEAST COMMON DENOMINATOR   Name _____

35	9	35	21	60	36	30	12	9	35
12	15	17	4	18	50	45	17	50	12
18	6	10	30	45	60	15	6	36	80
17	50	21	60	21	80	10	30	18	17
36	20	4	15	60	36	30	45	20	4
15	17	50	10	50	15	4	18	17	30
60	45	20	80	45	6	21	20	60	36
10	12	10	6	18	80	10	6	12	4
9	36	35	9	36	4	35	9	6	35
12	35	45	12	35	9	12	60	12	9

Find the least common denominator.

■ $\frac{1}{5}$ and $\frac{3}{7}$

◨ $\frac{1}{3}$ and $\frac{5}{21}$

◪ $\frac{7}{12}$ and $\frac{4}{5}$

◪ $\frac{1}{2}$ and $\frac{3}{4}$ ◧ $\frac{3}{4}$ and $\frac{5}{36}$ � $\frac{3}{10}$ and $\frac{2}{3}$ ◨ $\frac{4}{5}$ and $\frac{2}{3}$

◪ $\frac{5}{6}$ and $\frac{2}{3}$ ■ $\frac{1}{3}$ and $\frac{3}{4}$ ◣ $\frac{1}{2}$ and $\frac{3}{5}$ ◤ $\frac{3}{5}$ and $\frac{11}{80}$

◣ $\frac{4}{5}$ and $\frac{1}{9}$ ◺ $\frac{11}{25}$ and $\frac{9}{50}$ ■ $\frac{7}{9}$ and $\frac{1}{3}$ ◨ $\frac{1}{3}$ and $\frac{7}{18}$

20 RENAMING FRACTIONS Name _____

9	20	24	21	4	5	12	6	7	14
30	18	14	7	13	32	20	9	18	8
27	24	13	21	4	18	15	32	30	15
8	14	7	32	4	5	13	6	12	20
18	32	5	4	5	18	4	5	13	5
4	13	18	5	18	5	18	4	32	18
9	6	12	13	4	18	32	21	7	27
20	9	32	20	18	5	24	13	27	8
14	18	30	9	32	13	14	8	18	9
8	27	15	20	4	5	7	21	15	6

Find each missing numerator.

$\dfrac{2}{5} = \dfrac{\square}{10}$

$\dfrac{3}{8} = \dfrac{\square}{32}$

$\dfrac{2}{11} = \dfrac{\square}{33}$

$\dfrac{4}{9} = \dfrac{\square}{45}$ $\dfrac{1}{2} = \dfrac{\square}{16}$ $\dfrac{1}{3} = \dfrac{\square}{81}$ $\dfrac{3}{4} = \dfrac{\square}{20}$

$\dfrac{3}{5} = \dfrac{\square}{50}$ $\dfrac{6}{7} = \dfrac{\square}{21}$ $\dfrac{2}{3} = \dfrac{\square}{36}$ $\dfrac{7}{9} = \dfrac{\square}{27}$

$\dfrac{1}{2} = \dfrac{\square}{14}$ $\dfrac{2}{9} = \dfrac{\square}{63}$ $\dfrac{1}{6} = \dfrac{\square}{30}$ $\dfrac{1}{4} = \dfrac{\square}{36}$

21 ADDITION

$1\frac{7}{10}$	$\frac{13}{18}$	$1\frac{3}{4}$	$1\frac{1}{4}$	$\frac{7}{8}$	$1\frac{7}{10}$	$1\frac{1}{4}$	$\frac{5}{6}$	$1\frac{5}{24}$	$\frac{7}{8}$
$1\frac{4}{21}$	$1\frac{3}{40}$	$\frac{5}{6}$	$1\frac{3}{4}$	$\frac{31}{32}$	$1\frac{4}{21}$	$\frac{5}{6}$	$1\frac{3}{4}$	$1\frac{2}{15}$	$1\frac{1}{16}$
$1\frac{1}{7}$	$1\frac{5}{24}$	$\frac{7}{8}$	$\frac{5}{6}$	$1\frac{3}{4}$	$\frac{5}{6}$	$1\frac{3}{4}$	$1\frac{1}{4}$	$\frac{13}{18}$	$\frac{21}{22}$
$1\frac{1}{4}$	$1\frac{2}{15}$	$1\frac{1}{16}$	$\frac{13}{16}$	$\frac{21}{22}$	$1\frac{1}{5}$	$\frac{31}{32}$	$1\frac{4}{21}$	$1\frac{3}{5}$	$1\frac{7}{10}$
$\frac{7}{8}$	$\frac{13}{18}$	$\frac{5}{6}$	$1\frac{3}{5}$	$1\frac{4}{21}$	$1\frac{1}{16}$	$1\frac{2}{15}$	$1\frac{3}{4}$	$1\frac{1}{16}$	$1\frac{1}{4}$
$1\frac{7}{10}$	$1\frac{3}{4}$	$1\frac{3}{40}$	$1\frac{7}{10}$	$1\frac{1}{4}$	$\frac{7}{8}$	$1\frac{7}{10}$	$1\frac{1}{7}$	$\frac{5}{6}$	$\frac{7}{8}$
$\frac{7}{8}$	$1\frac{2}{15}$	$\frac{31}{32}$	$1\frac{4}{21}$	$1\frac{1}{16}$	$\frac{13}{18}$	$1\frac{5}{24}$	$\frac{13}{16}$	$\frac{21}{22}$	$1\frac{7}{10}$
$1\frac{2}{15}$	$\frac{31}{32}$	$1\frac{1}{7}$	$\frac{21}{22}$	$1\frac{2}{15}$	$1\frac{3}{5}$	$1\frac{1}{5}$	$1\frac{3}{40}$	$\frac{13}{16}$	$1\frac{3}{5}$
$1\frac{1}{4}$	$1\frac{1}{7}$	$1\frac{1}{16}$	$\frac{7}{8}$	$1\frac{7}{10}$	$1\frac{1}{4}$	$\frac{7}{8}$	$\frac{13}{18}$	$\frac{21}{22}$	$\frac{7}{8}$
$1\frac{7}{10}$	$\frac{7}{8}$	$1\frac{1}{5}$	$1\frac{5}{24}$	$1\frac{1}{4}$	$1\frac{7}{10}$	$1\frac{4}{21}$	$1\frac{3}{40}$	$1\frac{1}{4}$	$1\frac{7}{10}$

Reduce each answer if possible.

$\blacksquare$ $\quad \frac{1}{2}$
$+\frac{3}{8}$

◪ $\quad \frac{4}{9}$
$+\frac{5}{18}$

◩ $\quad \frac{3}{4}$
$+\frac{17}{20}$

◩ $\quad \frac{4}{11}$
$+\frac{13}{22}$

◸ $\quad \frac{5}{6}$
$+\frac{11}{30}$

◹ $\quad \frac{5}{16}$
$+\frac{3}{4}$

◸ $\quad \frac{16}{21}$
$+\frac{3}{7}$

◰ $\quad \frac{19}{40}$
$+\frac{3}{5}$

$\blacksquare$ $\quad \frac{2}{3}$
$+\frac{7}{12}$

◤ $\quad \frac{8}{15}$
$+\frac{3}{5}$

◸ $\quad \frac{5}{6}$
$+\frac{9}{24}$

◿ $\quad \frac{1}{2}$
$+\frac{9}{14}$

◺ $\quad \frac{19}{32}$
$+\frac{3}{8}$

$\blacksquare$ $\quad \frac{4}{5}$
$+\frac{9}{10}$

◩ $\quad \frac{7}{16}$
$+\frac{3}{8}$

Name _____

$\frac{10}{33}$	$\frac{10}{23}$	$\frac{10}{23}$	$\frac{7}{24}$	$1\frac{13}{30}$	$\frac{11}{18}$	$1\frac{11}{18}$	$\frac{10}{23}$	$1\frac{8}{9}$	$1\frac{11}{15}$
$\frac{7}{15}$	$\frac{11}{14}$	$1\frac{7}{20}$	$\frac{37}{56}$	$1\frac{5}{12}$	$1\frac{3}{10}$	$\frac{7}{15}$	$1\frac{7}{20}$	$\frac{11}{14}$	$\frac{19}{24}$
$1\frac{7}{20}$	$\frac{10}{33}$	$\frac{7}{24}$	$1\frac{2}{15}$	$1\frac{13}{30}$	$\frac{11}{18}$	$\frac{11}{14}$	$1\frac{11}{18}$	$1\frac{11}{15}$	$1\frac{2}{15}$
$\frac{11}{14}$	$\frac{19}{24}$	$1\frac{5}{12}$	$1\frac{7}{20}$	$1\frac{8}{9}$	$\frac{10}{23}$	$1\frac{2}{15}$	$\frac{37}{56}$	$\frac{23}{24}$	$1\frac{7}{20}$
$\frac{11}{18}$	$1\frac{7}{20}$	$\frac{11}{14}$	$1\frac{13}{30}$	$1\frac{5}{12}$	$1\frac{3}{10}$	$1\frac{11}{15}$	$1\frac{7}{20}$	$1\frac{2}{15}$	$1\frac{11}{18}$
$\frac{10}{23}$	$1\frac{8}{9}$	$1\frac{8}{9}$	$\frac{10}{23}$	$\frac{10}{33}$	$1\frac{11}{15}$	$1\frac{8}{9}$	$\frac{10}{23}$	$1\frac{8}{9}$	$1\frac{8}{9}$
$\frac{23}{24}$	$\frac{19}{24}$	$1\frac{5}{12}$	$\frac{19}{24}$	$\frac{7}{15}$	$\frac{37}{56}$	$1\frac{5}{12}$	$1\frac{3}{10}$	$\frac{23}{24}$	$\frac{37}{56}$
$\frac{11}{18}$	$1\frac{3}{10}$	$\frac{23}{24}$	$\frac{19}{24}$	$1\frac{5}{12}$	$1\frac{3}{10}$	$\frac{7}{15}$	$\frac{19}{24}$	$1\frac{5}{12}$	$1\frac{11}{18}$
$\frac{37}{56}$	$1\frac{11}{15}$	$\frac{10}{33}$	$\frac{7}{24}$	$1\frac{13}{30}$	$\frac{7}{24}$	$1\frac{11}{18}$	$\frac{11}{18}$	$\frac{10}{33}$	$\frac{7}{15}$
$\frac{11}{14}$	$\frac{19}{24}$	$1\frac{5}{12}$	$\frac{19}{24}$	$\frac{7}{15}$	$1\frac{3}{10}$	$\frac{23}{24}$	$\frac{37}{56}$	$1\frac{5}{12}$	$1\frac{7}{20}$

Reduce each answer if possible.

■ $\frac{2}{7}$
$+\frac{1}{2}$

◨ $\frac{1}{6}$
$+\frac{3}{22}$

◨ $\frac{1}{15}$
$+\frac{8}{20}$

◨ $\frac{2}{3}$
$+\frac{3}{4}$

◣ $\frac{3}{8}$
$+\frac{2}{7}$

◩ $\frac{1}{8}$
$+\frac{1}{6}$

◨ $\frac{7}{10}$
$+\frac{11}{15}$

◨ $\frac{1}{3}$
$+\frac{5}{8}$

■ $\frac{3}{5}$
$+\frac{3}{4}$

◩ $\frac{4}{5}$
$+\frac{1}{2}$

◩ $\frac{9}{10}$
$+\frac{5}{6}$

◣ $\frac{5}{12}$
$+\frac{3}{8}$

◪ $\frac{1}{2}$
$+\frac{1}{9}$

■ $\frac{5}{6}$
$+\frac{3}{10}$

◨ $\frac{7}{9}$
$+\frac{5}{6}$

Name _____

$\frac{9}{10}$	$\frac{15}{28}$	$\frac{2}{21}$	$\frac{13}{18}$	$\frac{8}{15}$	$\frac{2}{21}$	$\frac{13}{18}$	$\frac{8}{15}$	$\frac{9}{14}$	$\frac{9}{10}$
$\frac{5}{16}$	$\frac{5}{24}$	$\frac{3}{10}$	$\frac{1}{42}$	$\frac{15}{28}$	$\frac{7}{12}$	$\frac{15}{28}$	$\frac{9}{14}$	$\frac{1}{5}$	$\frac{7}{12}$
$\frac{13}{18}$	$\frac{3}{10}$	$\frac{2}{21}$	$\frac{7}{18}$	$\frac{13}{18}$	$\frac{8}{15}$	$\frac{5}{24}$	$\frac{2}{21}$	$\frac{1}{42}$	$\frac{2}{21}$
$\frac{8}{15}$	$\frac{1}{5}$	$\frac{7}{12}$	$\frac{2}{21}$	$\frac{19}{60}$	$\frac{1}{2}$	$\frac{13}{18}$	$\frac{5}{16}$	$\frac{1}{12}$	$\frac{13}{18}$
$\frac{2}{21}$	$\frac{5}{16}$	$\frac{13}{18}$	$\frac{1}{12}$	$\frac{5}{24}$	$\frac{1}{2}$	$\frac{1}{5}$	$\frac{8}{15}$	$\frac{1}{42}$	$\frac{8}{15}$
$\frac{13}{18}$	$\frac{7}{18}$	$\frac{8}{15}$	$\frac{9}{14}$	$\frac{7}{12}$	$\frac{15}{28}$	$\frac{5}{16}$	$\frac{2}{21}$	$\frac{19}{60}$	$\frac{2}{21}$
$\frac{8}{15}$	$\frac{15}{28}$	$\frac{5}{24}$	$\frac{13}{18}$	$\frac{1}{42}$	$\frac{3}{10}$	$\frac{8}{15}$	$\frac{7}{18}$	$\frac{7}{12}$	$\frac{13}{18}$
$\frac{2}{21}$	$\frac{1}{5}$	$\frac{8}{15}$	$\frac{3}{10}$	$\frac{2}{21}$	$\frac{13}{18}$	$\frac{9}{14}$	$\frac{2}{21}$	$\frac{5}{24}$	$\frac{8}{15}$
$\frac{1}{5}$	$\frac{1}{42}$	$\frac{1}{2}$	$\frac{1}{12}$	$\frac{7}{18}$	$\frac{19}{60}$	$\frac{1}{2}$	$\frac{1}{12}$	$\frac{5}{16}$	$\frac{19}{60}$
$\frac{9}{10}$	$\frac{1}{2}$	$\frac{13}{18}$	$\frac{2}{21}$	$\frac{8}{15}$	$\frac{13}{18}$	$\frac{2}{21}$	$\frac{8}{15}$	$\frac{5}{24}$	$\frac{9}{10}$

Reduce each answer if possible.

■ $\frac{3}{7}$ $-\frac{1}{3}$

◿ $\frac{3}{8}$ $-\frac{1}{6}$

◿ $\frac{4}{5}$ $-\frac{1}{2}$

◿ $\frac{3}{4}$ $-\frac{3}{14}$

◨ $\frac{24}{28}$ $-\frac{3}{14}$

◥ $\frac{1}{2}$ $-\frac{1}{9}$

◿ $\frac{3}{4}$ $-\frac{2}{3}$

◤ $\frac{5}{8}$ $-\frac{5}{16}$

■ $\frac{5}{6}$ $-\frac{1}{9}$

◤ $\frac{9}{14}$ $-\frac{13}{21}$

◥ $\frac{3}{5}$ $-\frac{1}{10}$

◤ $\frac{5}{6}$ $-\frac{1}{4}$

◹ $\frac{9}{15}$ $-\frac{2}{5}$

■ $\frac{7}{10}$ $-\frac{1}{6}$

◿ $\frac{11}{15}$ $-\frac{5}{12}$

24 ADDITION

$1\frac{3}{4}$	$1\frac{11}{12}$	$\frac{5}{6}$	$1\frac{2}{3}$	$1\frac{1}{3}$	$1\frac{7}{8}$	$1\frac{1}{2}$	$1\frac{5}{6}$	$1\frac{11}{12}$	$1\frac{11}{20}$
$1\frac{7}{8}$	$2\frac{2}{15}$	$1\frac{1}{5}$	$\frac{13}{24}$	$\frac{2}{3}$	$2\frac{1}{3}$	$1\frac{5}{12}$	$2\frac{1}{3}$	$1\frac{2}{3}$	$1\frac{1}{3}$
$1\frac{1}{5}$	$1\frac{11}{20}$	$1\frac{5}{6}$	$1\frac{5}{12}$	$3\frac{5}{8}$	$1\frac{6}{7}$	$\frac{13}{24}$	$\frac{5}{6}$	$1\frac{3}{4}$	$1\frac{1}{2}$
$3\frac{5}{8}$	$\frac{2}{3}$	$1\frac{3}{4}$	$1\frac{5}{6}$	$1\frac{6}{7}$	$3\frac{5}{8}$	$1\frac{11}{20}$	$\frac{13}{24}$	$2\frac{1}{3}$	$1\frac{6}{7}$
$1\frac{11}{20}$	$3\frac{5}{8}$	$1\frac{6}{7}$	$1\frac{2}{3}$	$1\frac{1}{3}$	$1\frac{11}{12}$	$2\frac{1}{3}$	$1\frac{6}{7}$	$3\frac{5}{8}$	$1\frac{5}{6}$
$1\frac{1}{2}$	$1\frac{5}{12}$	$1\frac{7}{8}$	$1\frac{11}{20}$	$\frac{2}{3}$	$2\frac{2}{15}$	$1\frac{3}{4}$	$1\frac{1}{3}$	$\frac{5}{6}$	$\frac{2}{3}$
$1\frac{6}{7}$	$1\frac{11}{12}$	$2\frac{1}{3}$	$1\frac{1}{5}$	$\frac{13}{24}$	$1\frac{5}{6}$	$1\frac{1}{2}$	$1\frac{1}{5}$	$1\frac{7}{8}$	$1\frac{6}{7}$
$\frac{13}{24}$	$1\frac{2}{3}$	$1\frac{11}{20}$	$1\frac{6}{7}$	$\frac{2}{3}$	$2\frac{1}{3}$	$1\frac{6}{7}$	$1\frac{5}{12}$	$2\frac{2}{15}$	$1\frac{3}{4}$
$1\frac{11}{12}$	$\frac{5}{6}$	$\frac{2}{3}$	$\frac{5}{6}$	$1\frac{6}{7}$	$3\frac{5}{8}$	$1\frac{3}{4}$	$2\frac{1}{3}$	$1\frac{5}{6}$	$1\frac{7}{8}$
$1\frac{7}{8}$	$1\frac{1}{3}$	$1\frac{11}{20}$	$1\frac{1}{5}$	$\frac{13}{24}$	$1\frac{5}{6}$	$2\frac{2}{15}$	$1\frac{5}{12}$	$1\frac{11}{12}$	$1\frac{1}{3}$

Reduce each answer if possible.

$$\begin{array}{r} \frac{3}{4} \\ \frac{1}{2} \\ +\ \frac{2}{3} \\ \hline \end{array}$$

$$\begin{array}{r} \frac{3}{5} \\ \frac{5}{6} \\ +\ \frac{7}{10} \\ \hline \end{array}$$

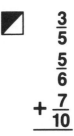

$$\begin{array}{r} \frac{1}{4} \\ \frac{2}{3} \\ +\ \frac{5}{6} \\ \hline \end{array}$$

$$\begin{array}{r} \frac{1}{3} \\ \frac{6}{7} \\ +\ \frac{9}{14} \\ \hline \end{array}$$

$$\begin{array}{r} \frac{5}{12} \\ \frac{1}{6} \\ +\ \frac{2}{8} \\ \hline \end{array}$$

$$\begin{array}{r} \frac{7}{10} \\ \frac{1}{3} \\ +\ \frac{1}{6} \\ \hline \end{array}$$

$$\begin{array}{r} \frac{3}{4} \\ \frac{11}{12} \\ +\ \frac{2}{3} \\ \hline \end{array}$$

$$\begin{array}{r} \frac{2}{8} \\ \frac{1}{2} \\ +\ \frac{2}{3} \\ \hline \end{array}$$

$$\begin{array}{r} \frac{1}{6} \\ \frac{2}{3} \\ +\ \frac{1}{2} \\ \hline \end{array}$$

$$\begin{array}{r} \frac{1}{4} \\ \frac{3}{5} \\ +\ \frac{7}{10} \\ \hline \end{array}$$

$$\begin{array}{r} \frac{1}{4} \\ \frac{5}{6} \\ +\ \frac{7}{12} \\ \hline \end{array}$$

$$\begin{array}{r} \frac{1}{6} \\ \frac{1}{4} \\ +\ \frac{1}{8} \\ \hline \end{array}$$

$$\begin{array}{r} \frac{1}{5} \\ \frac{3}{10} \\ +\ \frac{1}{6} \\ \hline \end{array}$$

$$\begin{array}{r} \frac{3}{4} \\ \frac{1}{2} \\ +\ \frac{5}{8} \\ \hline \end{array}$$

$$\begin{array}{r} \frac{5}{6} \\ \frac{1}{4} \\ +\ \frac{5}{12} \\ \hline \end{array}$$

Name _____

18	$1\frac{5}{24}$	10	$1\frac{8}{21}$	12	35	10	$\frac{23}{30}$	$\frac{13}{45}$	$1\frac{8}{21}$
$\frac{7}{15}$	24	21	$1\frac{7}{9}$	$1\frac{2}{15}$	18	$1\frac{7}{9}$	$1\frac{2}{15}$	35	$1\frac{5}{9}$
12	35	12	24	$1\frac{5}{9}$	$\frac{15}{16}$	35	12	24	12
35	24	$1\frac{7}{9}$	$\frac{15}{16}$	35	12	$\frac{4}{7}$	$1\frac{7}{9}$	35	24
12	$1\frac{7}{9}$	$\frac{7}{15}$	10	$1\frac{8}{21}$	21	$1\frac{2}{15}$	$1\frac{5}{9}$	$1\frac{7}{9}$	35
24	$1\frac{5}{24}$	18	$\frac{15}{16}$	$1\frac{7}{9}$	$1\frac{7}{9}$	$1\frac{5}{9}$	$\frac{23}{30}$	$\frac{13}{45}$	24
35	21	$\frac{7}{15}$	24	10	$1\frac{2}{15}$	35	$\frac{13}{45}$	$1\frac{8}{21}$	12
12	$\frac{4}{7}$	$1\frac{8}{21}$	$\frac{23}{30}$	$\frac{4}{7}$	$1\frac{5}{24}$	18	21	$\frac{7}{15}$	35
$1\frac{2}{15}$	24	$1\frac{5}{9}$	$\frac{7}{15}$	35	12	$1\frac{5}{9}$	$\frac{15}{16}$	24	18
$\frac{13}{45}$	$1\frac{8}{21}$	35	12	24	35	24	12	10	$\frac{15}{16}$

■ Find the least common denominator.

$$\frac{3}{4} \text{ and } \frac{1}{3}$$

◪ Find the missing numerator.

$$\frac{3}{4} = \frac{\square}{24}$$

◪
$$\frac{5}{6}$$
$$+\frac{3}{8}$$

◪
$$\frac{1}{6}$$
$$+\frac{3}{10}$$

◪
$$\frac{10}{14}$$
$$-\frac{1}{7}$$

◪
$$\frac{4}{5}$$
$$+\frac{1}{3}$$

◪ Find the missing numerator.

$$\frac{5}{7} = \frac{\square}{14}$$

◪
$$\frac{3}{8}$$
$$+\frac{9}{16}$$

■ Find the least common denominator.

$$\frac{3}{5} \text{ and } \frac{4}{7}$$

◪
$$\frac{3}{4}$$
$$\frac{5}{12}$$
$$+\frac{7}{18}$$

◪
$$\frac{2}{3}$$
$$+\frac{5}{7}$$

◪
$$\frac{11}{15}$$
$$-\frac{4}{9}$$

◪
$$\frac{1}{6}$$
$$+\frac{3}{5}$$

■ Find the least common denominator.

$$\frac{1}{8} \text{ and } \frac{3}{12}$$

◪ Find the missing numerator.

$$\frac{7}{18} = \frac{\square}{54}$$

Name _____

$4\frac{13}{20}$	$5\frac{7}{16}$	$7\frac{11}{42}$	$9\frac{5}{6}$	$12\frac{11}{14}$	$11\frac{1}{2}$	$6\frac{1}{2}$	$5\frac{7}{16}$	$7\frac{11}{42}$	$12\frac{11}{14}$
$3\frac{13}{24}$	$11\frac{1}{2}$	$4\frac{5}{8}$	$3\frac{1}{2}$	$6\frac{1}{2}$	$6\frac{5}{9}$	$3\frac{13}{24}$	$3\frac{17}{35}$	$12\frac{11}{14}$	$3\frac{1}{2}$
$3\frac{17}{35}$	$11\frac{1}{2}$	$12\frac{11}{14}$	$3\frac{5}{6}$	$3\frac{15}{16}$	$9\frac{13}{30}$	$11\frac{1}{2}$	$4\frac{13}{20}$	$3\frac{5}{6}$	$4\frac{5}{8}$
$7\frac{11}{42}$	$3\frac{15}{16}$	$9\frac{13}{30}$	$5\frac{7}{16}$	$11\frac{1}{2}$	$3\frac{5}{6}$	$3\frac{1}{2}$	$3\frac{15}{16}$	$9\frac{13}{30}$	$3\frac{13}{24}$
$4\frac{5}{8}$	$3\frac{1}{2}$	$3\frac{13}{24}$	$3\frac{17}{35}$	$4\frac{13}{20}$	$12\frac{11}{14}$	$4\frac{5}{8}$	$7\frac{11}{42}$	$5\frac{7}{16}$	$11\frac{1}{2}$
$3\frac{1}{2}$	$3\frac{5}{6}$	$6\frac{3}{4}$	$9\frac{5}{6}$	$6\frac{1}{2}$	$6\frac{5}{9}$	$6\frac{1}{2}$	$6\frac{3}{4}$	$3\frac{17}{35}$	$5\frac{7}{16}$
$3\frac{17}{35}$	$9\frac{13}{30}$	$6\frac{3}{4}$	$6\frac{5}{9}$	$3\frac{15}{16}$	$9\frac{13}{30}$	$6\frac{5}{9}$	$6\frac{3}{4}$	$3\frac{15}{16}$	$4\frac{5}{8}$
$6\frac{1}{2}$	$12\frac{11}{14}$	$6\frac{3}{4}$	$5\frac{7}{16}$	$3\frac{1}{2}$	$3\frac{13}{24}$	$7\frac{11}{42}$	$6\frac{3}{4}$	$4\frac{13}{20}$	$6\frac{1}{2}$
$3\frac{15}{16}$	$6\frac{5}{9}$	$4\frac{5}{8}$	$11\frac{1}{2}$	$3\frac{5}{6}$	$4\frac{13}{20}$	$3\frac{5}{6}$	$3\frac{17}{35}$	$6\frac{5}{9}$	$3\frac{13}{24}$
$6\frac{3}{4}$	$7\frac{11}{42}$	$9\frac{5}{6}$	$5\frac{7}{16}$	$3\frac{1}{2}$	$9\frac{13}{30}$	$3\frac{15}{16}$	$9\frac{5}{6}$	$9\frac{13}{30}$	$6\frac{3}{4}$

Reduce each answer if possible.

■ $\quad 7\frac{1}{12}$
$\quad +2\frac{3}{4}$

◳ $\quad 3\frac{1}{4}$
$\quad +2\frac{3}{16}$

◲ $\quad 6\frac{4}{11}$
$\quad +5\frac{3}{22}$

◩ $\quad 3\frac{1}{5}$
$\quad +\ \ \frac{2}{7}$

◤ $\quad 5\frac{5}{7}$
$\quad +7\frac{1}{14}$

◨ $\quad 3\frac{5}{42}$
$\quad +4\frac{1}{7}$

◳ $\quad \frac{3}{8}$
$\quad +3\frac{1}{6}$

◩ $\quad 2\frac{2}{5}$
$\quad +2\frac{1}{4}$

■ $\quad 1\frac{3}{10}$
$\quad +5\frac{1}{5}$

� $\quad 1\frac{3}{8}$
$\quad +3\frac{3}{12}$

◫ $\quad 3\frac{3}{14}$
$\quad +\ \ \frac{2}{7}$

◺ $\quad \frac{1}{3}$
$\quad +3\frac{1}{2}$

◳ $\quad 1\frac{5}{16}$
$\quad +2\frac{5}{8}$

■ $\quad 6\frac{1}{3}$
$\quad +\ \ \frac{2}{9}$

◨ $\quad 5\frac{3}{10}$
$\quad +4\frac{2}{15}$

27 ADDITION

$8\frac{17}{24}$	$9\frac{1}{2}$	$6\frac{7}{10}$	$5\frac{7}{10}$	$6\frac{7}{30}$	$8\frac{4}{7}$	$8\frac{13}{21}$	$9\frac{13}{21}$	$9\frac{11}{14}$	$3\frac{5}{36}$
$5\frac{2}{3}$	$5\frac{5}{8}$	$4\frac{2}{3}$	$6\frac{9}{20}$	$5\frac{9}{20}$	$4\frac{2}{3}$	$7\frac{7}{25}$	$5\frac{9}{20}$	$5\frac{5}{8}$	$7\frac{2}{15}$
$9\frac{13}{21}$	$8\frac{13}{21}$	$6\frac{7}{10}$	$5\frac{5}{8}$	$4\frac{2}{3}$	$5\frac{7}{10}$	$9\frac{13}{21}$	$6\frac{7}{10}$	$8\frac{13}{21}$	$6\frac{7}{10}$
$6\frac{5}{18}$	$6\frac{9}{20}$	$9\frac{13}{21}$	$6\frac{7}{10}$	$4\frac{7}{12}$	$5\frac{2}{3}$	$5\frac{5}{8}$	$6\frac{7}{10}$	$8\frac{4}{7}$	$6\frac{2}{15}$
$6\frac{7}{30}$	$5\frac{7}{30}$	$7\frac{4}{7}$	$8\frac{4}{7}$	$8\frac{17}{24}$	$8\frac{4}{7}$	$6\frac{9}{20}$	$7\frac{4}{7}$	$5\frac{7}{30}$	$3\frac{5}{36}$
$7\frac{2}{15}$	$6\frac{2}{15}$	$5\frac{9}{20}$	$7\frac{5}{18}$	$4\frac{7}{12}$	$9\frac{1}{2}$	$7\frac{2}{15}$	$5\frac{9}{20}$	$6\frac{2}{15}$	$5\frac{2}{3}$
$8\frac{13}{21}$	$4\frac{7}{12}$	$5\frac{5}{8}$	$9\frac{13}{21}$	$8\frac{17}{24}$	$7\frac{7}{25}$	$9\frac{13}{21}$	$5\frac{5}{8}$	$9\frac{1}{2}$	$8\frac{13}{21}$
$5\frac{5}{8}$	$6\frac{5}{18}$	$6\frac{7}{10}$	$5\frac{5}{8}$	$5\frac{7}{30}$	$7\frac{4}{7}$	$5\frac{5}{8}$	$6\frac{7}{10}$	$6\frac{5}{18}$	$6\frac{7}{10}$
$8\frac{4}{7}$	$6\frac{7}{10}$	$6\frac{2}{15}$	$7\frac{2}{15}$	$8\frac{13}{21}$	$5\frac{9}{20}$	$7\frac{5}{18}$	$5\frac{7}{30}$	$5\frac{5}{8}$	$8\frac{17}{24}$
$9\frac{11}{14}$	$7\frac{7}{25}$	$9\frac{13}{21}$	$5\frac{7}{10}$	$9\frac{11}{14}$	$5\frac{2}{3}$	$4\frac{2}{3}$	$6\frac{7}{10}$	$6\frac{9}{20}$	$5\frac{2}{3}$

Reduce each answer if possible.

■ $3\frac{9}{10}$
  $+2\frac{4}{5}$

◩ $7\frac{7}{8}$
  $+\ \frac{5}{6}$

◪ $6\frac{6}{7}$
  $+2\frac{9}{14}$

◤ $3\frac{7}{9}$
  $+1\frac{24}{27}$

◥ $1\frac{20}{21}$
  $+7\frac{5}{6}$

◸ $\frac{7}{12}$
  $+2\frac{5}{9}$

◩ $5\frac{1}{3}$
  $+\ \frac{9}{10}$

◤ $6\frac{2}{3}$
  $+\ \frac{11}{18}$

■ $4\frac{7}{8}$
  $+\ \frac{3}{4}$

◤ $2\frac{5}{6}$
  $+1\frac{3}{4}$

◱ $4\frac{4}{5}$
  $+3\frac{27}{35}$

◤ $4\frac{3}{5}$
  $+2\frac{8}{15}$

◿ $5\frac{17}{25}$
  $+1\frac{3}{5}$

■ $3\frac{5}{7}$
  $+5\frac{19}{21}$

◨ $3\frac{3}{5}$
  $+2\frac{17}{20}$

Name _____

$5\frac{1}{3}$	$5\frac{5}{9}$	$6\frac{7}{15}$	$9\frac{1}{8}$	$3\frac{10}{21}$	$8\frac{10}{21}$	$9\frac{1}{8}$	$7\frac{11}{16}$	$7\frac{1}{12}$	$5\frac{5}{9}$
$7\frac{1}{12}$	$4\frac{1}{6}$	$1\frac{7}{16}$	$3\frac{3}{8}$	$9\frac{1}{8}$	$9\frac{1}{8}$	$2\frac{5}{24}$	$4\frac{7}{10}$	$5\frac{19}{60}$	$5\frac{1}{3}$
$4\frac{7}{10}$	$9\frac{1}{8}$	$9\frac{3}{4}$	$5\frac{19}{60}$	$7\frac{1}{5}$	$10\frac{1}{9}$	$4\frac{1}{6}$	$9\frac{1}{8}$	$9\frac{3}{4}$	$1\frac{7}{16}$
$6\frac{7}{15}$	$2\frac{5}{24}$	$3\frac{3}{8}$	$7\frac{11}{16}$	$5\frac{5}{9}$	$5\frac{1}{3}$	$7\frac{1}{5}$	$2\frac{5}{24}$	$3\frac{3}{8}$	$7\frac{11}{16}$
$5\frac{1}{3}$	$8\frac{10}{21}$	$1\frac{7}{16}$	$7\frac{1}{12}$	$4\frac{7}{10}$	$3\frac{10}{21}$	$7\frac{1}{12}$	$4\frac{7}{10}$	$3\frac{10}{21}$	$5\frac{1}{3}$
$7\frac{1}{12}$	$6\frac{7}{15}$	$9\frac{3}{4}$	$9\frac{1}{8}$	$9\frac{3}{4}$	$9\frac{1}{8}$	$9\frac{3}{4}$	$9\frac{1}{8}$	$10\frac{1}{9}$	$5\frac{5}{9}$
$5\frac{5}{9}$	$1\frac{7}{16}$	$3\frac{3}{8}$	$1\frac{7}{16}$	$7\frac{1}{12}$	$5\frac{1}{3}$	$4\frac{1}{6}$	$7\frac{11}{16}$	$4\frac{1}{6}$	$7\frac{1}{12}$
$5\frac{1}{3}$	$7\frac{1}{5}$	$5\frac{19}{60}$	$7\frac{1}{5}$	$5\frac{19}{60}$	$8\frac{10}{21}$	$2\frac{5}{24}$	$4\frac{7}{10}$	$2\frac{5}{24}$	$5\frac{1}{3}$
$3\frac{10}{21}$	$7\frac{1}{12}$	$3\frac{3}{8}$	$3\frac{10}{21}$	$7\frac{1}{5}$	$10\frac{1}{9}$	$8\frac{10}{21}$	$7\frac{11}{16}$	$5\frac{5}{9}$	$4\frac{1}{6}$
$6\frac{7}{15}$	$5\frac{19}{60}$	$5\frac{5}{9}$	$5\frac{1}{3}$	$7\frac{1}{12}$	$5\frac{5}{9}$	$5\frac{1}{3}$	$7\frac{1}{12}$	$4\frac{7}{10}$	$2\frac{5}{24}$

Reduce each answer if possible.

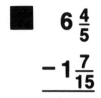 $6\frac{4}{5}$
$-1\frac{7}{15}$

◨ $5\frac{2}{3}$
$-1\frac{1}{2}$

◩ $10\frac{7}{8}$
$-3\frac{3}{16}$

◪ $9\frac{1}{3}$
$-7\frac{1}{8}$

◳ $9\frac{5}{6}$
$-3\frac{11}{30}$

◰ $10\frac{2}{3}$
$-7\frac{4}{21}$

◪ $7\frac{5}{6}$
$-3\frac{2}{15}$

◧ $11\frac{2}{3}$
$-1\frac{5}{9}$

■ $8\frac{8}{9}$
$-3\frac{1}{3}$

◸ $8\frac{7}{10}$
$-1\frac{1}{2}$

◳ $6\frac{11}{16}$
$-5\frac{1}{4}$

◺ $6\frac{5}{8}$
$-3\frac{3}{12}$

◳ $8\frac{5}{12}$
$-3\frac{1}{10}$

■ $8\frac{11}{12}$
$-1\frac{5}{6}$

◪ $9\frac{5}{7}$
$-1\frac{5}{21}$

Name _____

$9\frac{2}{15}$	$8\frac{3}{14}$	$5\frac{10}{21}$	$9\frac{7}{20}$	$9\frac{1}{2}$	$8\frac{7}{8}$	$1\frac{15}{28}$	$2\frac{17}{30}$	$7\frac{26}{35}$	$7\frac{1}{3}$
$3\frac{21}{22}$	$1\frac{15}{28}$	$5\frac{4}{9}$	$9\frac{2}{15}$	$2\frac{17}{30}$	$2\frac{1}{2}$	$9\frac{2}{15}$	$7\frac{1}{3}$	$3\frac{7}{18}$	$6\frac{23}{24}$
$2\frac{1}{2}$	$7\frac{1}{3}$	$8\frac{7}{8}$	$9\frac{1}{2}$	$7\frac{1}{3}$	$5\frac{4}{9}$	$3\frac{21}{22}$	$7\frac{26}{35}$	$5\frac{4}{9}$	$9\frac{7}{20}$
$9\frac{1}{2}$	$5\frac{4}{9}$	$1\frac{15}{28}$	$3\frac{7}{18}$	$7\frac{26}{35}$	$8\frac{3}{14}$	$1\frac{15}{28}$	$9\frac{7}{20}$	$7\frac{1}{3}$	$3\frac{21}{22}$
$2\frac{17}{30}$	$7\frac{26}{35}$	$3\frac{21}{22}$	$9\frac{1}{2}$	$2\frac{17}{30}$	$5\frac{10}{21}$	$8\frac{3}{14}$	$6\frac{23}{24}$	$8\frac{7}{8}$	$2\frac{1}{2}$
$8\frac{7}{8}$	$2\frac{1}{2}$	$9\frac{7}{20}$	$5\frac{10}{21}$	$3\frac{21}{22}$	$7\frac{26}{35}$	$2\frac{17}{30}$	$1\frac{15}{28}$	$3\frac{7}{18}$	$7\frac{26}{35}$
$1\frac{15}{28}$	$5\frac{4}{9}$	$6\frac{23}{24}$	$8\frac{3}{14}$	$1\frac{15}{28}$	$9\frac{7}{20}$	$9\frac{1}{2}$	$8\frac{7}{8}$	$5\frac{4}{9}$	$3\frac{7}{18}$
$9\frac{1}{2}$	$9\frac{2}{15}$	$9\frac{7}{20}$	$5\frac{10}{21}$	$5\frac{4}{9}$	$7\frac{1}{3}$	$2\frac{17}{30}$	$1\frac{15}{28}$	$9\frac{2}{15}$	$8\frac{7}{8}$
$3\frac{7}{18}$	$7\frac{26}{35}$	$7\frac{1}{3}$	$9\frac{2}{15}$	$3\frac{21}{22}$	$7\frac{26}{35}$	$7\frac{1}{3}$	$5\frac{4}{9}$	$8\frac{3}{14}$	$5\frac{10}{21}$
$5\frac{4}{9}$	$2\frac{17}{30}$	$6\frac{23}{24}$	$8\frac{3}{14}$	$2\frac{1}{2}$	$2\frac{17}{30}$	$9\frac{1}{2}$	$8\frac{7}{8}$	$2\frac{1}{2}$	$7\frac{1}{3}$

Reduce each answer if possible.

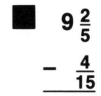

$$9\frac{2}{5} - \frac{4}{15}$$

$$8\frac{3}{7} - \frac{3}{14}$$

$$6\frac{3}{7} - \frac{20}{21}$$

$$2\frac{2}{7} - \frac{3}{4}$$

$$9\frac{3}{4} - \frac{2}{5}$$

$$10\frac{1}{5} - \frac{7}{10}$$

$$4\frac{5}{11} - \frac{11}{22}$$

$$3\frac{1}{3} - \frac{5}{6}$$

$$8\frac{1}{4} - \frac{11}{12}$$

$$4\frac{1}{6} - \frac{7}{9}$$

$$7\frac{5}{6} - \frac{7}{8}$$

$$3\frac{2}{5} - \frac{5}{6}$$

$$8\frac{3}{5} - \frac{6}{7}$$

$$6\frac{1}{9} - \frac{2}{3}$$

$$9\frac{3}{4} - \frac{7}{8}$$

Name _____

$1\frac{1}{2}$	$4\frac{7}{18}$	$2\frac{13}{14}$	$1\frac{17}{20}$	$1\frac{13}{16}$	$5\frac{9}{10}$	$1\frac{1}{2}$	$1\frac{5}{6}$	$3\frac{19}{24}$	$3\frac{21}{22}$
$2\frac{31}{35}$	$3\frac{21}{22}$	$3\frac{19}{24}$	$2\frac{31}{35}$	$7\frac{3}{8}$	$4\frac{10}{21}$	$\frac{14}{15}$	$4\frac{7}{18}$	$2\frac{5}{9}$	$1\frac{5}{6}$
$4\frac{10}{21}$	$8\frac{3}{8}$	$7\frac{3}{8}$	$2\frac{5}{9}$	$1\frac{5}{6}$	$2\frac{13}{14}$	$1\frac{17}{20}$	$2\frac{5}{9}$	$2\frac{13}{16}$	$7\frac{3}{8}$
$2\frac{5}{6}$	$\frac{14}{15}$	$3\frac{19}{24}$	$\frac{14}{15}$	$4\frac{11}{12}$	$5\frac{9}{10}$	$2\frac{13}{14}$	$4\frac{7}{18}$	$2\frac{31}{35}$	$5\frac{7}{18}$
$1\frac{5}{6}$	$1\frac{1}{2}$	$7\frac{3}{8}$	$2\frac{5}{9}$	$7\frac{3}{8}$	$1\frac{1}{2}$	$3\frac{21}{22}$	$4\frac{10}{21}$	$1\frac{17}{20}$	$2\frac{13}{14}$
$7\frac{3}{8}$	$3\frac{19}{24}$	$5\frac{7}{18}$	$5\frac{11}{12}$	$3\frac{5}{9}$	$2\frac{13}{16}$	$3\frac{13}{14}$	$8\frac{3}{8}$	$\frac{14}{15}$	$4\frac{10}{21}$
$2\frac{13}{14}$	$3\frac{21}{22}$	$2\frac{31}{35}$	$\frac{14}{15}$	$3\frac{19}{24}$	$4\frac{7}{18}$	$2\frac{31}{35}$	$1\frac{5}{6}$	$1\frac{1}{2}$	$4\frac{7}{18}$
$3\frac{21}{22}$	$3\frac{19}{24}$	$1\frac{17}{20}$	$4\frac{10}{21}$	$7\frac{3}{8}$	$1\frac{1}{2}$	$1\frac{17}{20}$	$2\frac{5}{9}$	$\frac{14}{15}$	$4\frac{10}{21}$
$2\frac{31}{35}$	$1\frac{17}{20}$	$2\frac{13}{14}$	$2\frac{31}{35}$	$2\frac{31}{35}$	$4\frac{7}{18}$	$1\frac{5}{6}$	$4\frac{7}{18}$	$2\frac{5}{9}$	$\frac{14}{15}$
$4\frac{11}{12}$	$2\frac{13}{14}$	$1\frac{17}{20}$	$3\frac{19}{24}$	$2\frac{13}{14}$	$1\frac{5}{6}$	$4\frac{7}{18}$	$4\frac{10}{21}$	$\frac{14}{15}$	$1\frac{13}{16}$

Reduce each answer if possible.

■ $4\frac{3}{8}$

$-2\frac{9}{16}$

◩ $6\frac{3}{7}$

$-1\frac{20}{21}$

◪ $5\frac{11}{15}$

$-4\frac{4}{5}$

◩ $8\frac{2}{9}$ ◤ $6\frac{3}{5}$ ◱ $11\frac{1}{4}$ ◩ $16\frac{2}{5}$

$-3\frac{5}{6}$ $-3\frac{5}{7}$ $-3\frac{7}{8}$ $-14\frac{9}{10}$

◩ $6\frac{1}{2}$ ■ $7\frac{4}{5}$ ◥ $5\frac{2}{3}$ ◪ $4\frac{1}{4}$

$-4\frac{2}{3}$ $-1\frac{9}{10}$ $-1\frac{7}{8}$ $-2\frac{2}{5}$

◥ $7\frac{3}{7}$ ◪ $6\frac{5}{11}$ ■ $8\frac{2}{3}$ ◩ $7\frac{2}{9}$

$-4\frac{1}{2}$ $-2\frac{11}{22}$ $-3\frac{3}{4}$ $-4\frac{2}{3}$

Name _____

$7\frac{3}{4}$	$7\frac{9}{40}$	$9\frac{7}{15}$	$8\frac{13}{18}$	$5\frac{7}{8}$	$2\frac{2}{3}$	$6\frac{1}{6}$	$8\frac{9}{10}$	$7\frac{3}{40}$	$7\frac{3}{4}$
$5\frac{1}{2}$	$5\frac{7}{8}$	$7\frac{9}{40}$	$2\frac{2}{3}$	$4\frac{11}{12}$	$6\frac{1}{2}$	$2\frac{2}{3}$	$9\frac{7}{8}$	$5\frac{7}{8}$	$9\frac{7}{8}$
$8\frac{9}{10}$	$5\frac{1}{2}$	$7\frac{3}{4}$	$5\frac{1}{2}$	$9\frac{7}{15}$	$8\frac{9}{10}$	$9\frac{7}{8}$	$7\frac{3}{4}$	$6\frac{1}{6}$	$9\frac{7}{15}$
$8\frac{13}{18}$	$5\frac{7}{8}$	$8\frac{13}{18}$	$7\frac{9}{40}$	$7\frac{3}{4}$	$9\frac{7}{15}$	$7\frac{3}{40}$	$6\frac{1}{6}$	$2\frac{2}{3}$	$7\frac{3}{40}$
$8\frac{2}{3}$	$4\frac{1}{9}$	$7\frac{3}{4}$	$9\frac{7}{15}$	$5\frac{1}{2}$	$6\frac{1}{6}$	$8\frac{9}{10}$	$7\frac{3}{4}$	$7\frac{1}{22}$	$5\frac{7}{8}$
$5\frac{7}{8}$	$9\frac{7}{8}$	$8\frac{9}{10}$	$7\frac{3}{4}$	$3\frac{9}{10}$	$9\frac{2}{3}$	$9\frac{7}{15}$	$8\frac{9}{10}$	$5\frac{1}{2}$	$2\frac{2}{3}$
$3\frac{9}{10}$	$3\frac{2}{3}$	$6\frac{1}{2}$	$3\frac{9}{10}$	$9\frac{7}{15}$	$8\frac{9}{10}$	$4\frac{11}{12}$	$9\frac{2}{3}$	$5\frac{7}{8}$	$4\frac{1}{9}$
$9\frac{7}{15}$	$7\frac{1}{22}$	$9\frac{7}{15}$	$7\frac{1}{22}$	$7\frac{3}{4}$	$9\frac{7}{15}$	$4\frac{1}{9}$	$9\frac{7}{15}$	$9\frac{2}{3}$	$8\frac{9}{10}$
$3\frac{9}{10}$	$5\frac{7}{8}$	$6\frac{1}{2}$	$2\frac{2}{3}$	$7\frac{3}{40}$	$7\frac{9}{40}$	$2\frac{2}{3}$	$4\frac{11}{12}$	$5\frac{7}{8}$	$4\frac{1}{9}$
$8\frac{9}{10}$	$7\frac{1}{22}$	$7\frac{3}{4}$	$3\frac{9}{10}$	$5\frac{7}{8}$	$5\frac{7}{8}$	$4\frac{1}{9}$	$7\frac{3}{4}$	$9\frac{2}{3}$	$9\frac{7}{15}$

Reduce each answer if possible.

■ $5\frac{1}{4}$
$+2\frac{1}{2}$

◢ $3\frac{3}{5}$
$+3\frac{5}{8}$

◪ $10\frac{2}{5}$
$-\frac{11}{15}$

◥ $6\frac{3}{4}$
$-1\frac{5}{6}$

◤ $7\frac{1}{3}$
$-\frac{5}{6}$

◸ $5\frac{1}{2}$
$+\frac{2}{3}$

◹ $6\frac{1}{10}$
$-\frac{3}{5}$

◿ $7\frac{1}{3}$
$-3\frac{2}{9}$

■ $5\frac{2}{3}$
$+3\frac{4}{5}$

◤ $8\frac{1}{5}$
$-4\frac{3}{10}$

◸ $4\frac{3}{8}$
$+2\frac{7}{10}$

◣ $6\frac{5}{11}$
$+\frac{13}{22}$

◹ $10\frac{1}{4}$
$-\frac{3}{8}$

■ $7\frac{3}{5}$
$+1\frac{3}{10}$

◿ $9\frac{5}{9}$
$-\frac{5}{6}$

Name _____

$5\frac{2}{5}$	$1\frac{1}{6}$	$\frac{5}{16}$	$\frac{5}{16}$	$8\frac{1}{4}$	$5\frac{2}{3}$	$\frac{5}{16}$	$1\frac{1}{6}$	$\frac{5}{16}$	$5\frac{2}{5}$
$1\frac{1}{6}$	$5\frac{2}{5}$	$5\frac{2}{3}$	$3\frac{5}{8}$	$4\frac{5}{12}$	$15\frac{3}{8}$	$1\frac{1}{8}$	$3\frac{5}{8}$	$5\frac{2}{5}$	$\frac{5}{16}$
$5\frac{2}{5}$	$2\frac{9}{16}$	$7\frac{1}{4}$	$1\frac{5}{16}$	$5\frac{2}{5}$	$\frac{5}{16}$	$6\frac{3}{5}$	$3\frac{5}{12}$	$4\frac{5}{12}$	$1\frac{1}{6}$
$5\frac{2}{5}$	$8\frac{1}{4}$	$1\frac{5}{16}$	$\frac{5}{16}$	$3\frac{5}{8}$	$1\frac{1}{6}$	$5\frac{2}{5}$	$1\frac{5}{16}$	$1\frac{1}{8}$	$\frac{5}{16}$
$3\frac{5}{8}$	$4\frac{3}{16}$	$1\frac{1}{6}$	$8\frac{1}{4}$	$5\frac{2}{5}$	$7\frac{1}{4}$	$\frac{5}{16}$	$1\frac{1}{6}$	$15\frac{3}{8}$	$5\frac{2}{3}$
$2\frac{9}{16}$	$1\frac{1}{8}$	$5\frac{2}{5}$	$1\frac{1}{6}$	$6\frac{3}{5}$	$\frac{5}{16}$	$3\frac{7}{12}$	$1\frac{1}{6}$	$8\frac{1}{4}$	$4\frac{3}{16}$
$\frac{5}{16}$	$15\frac{3}{8}$	$1\frac{5}{16}$	$5\frac{2}{5}$	$1\frac{1}{6}$	$3\frac{7}{12}$	$\frac{5}{16}$	$3\frac{5}{12}$	$4\frac{5}{12}$	$5\frac{2}{5}$
$1\frac{1}{6}$	$3\frac{5}{8}$	$3\frac{5}{12}$	$7\frac{1}{4}$	$\frac{5}{16}$	$5\frac{2}{5}$	$6\frac{3}{5}$	$1\frac{5}{16}$	$1\frac{1}{8}$	$1\frac{1}{6}$
$1\frac{1}{6}$	$\frac{5}{16}$	$4\frac{5}{12}$	$2\frac{9}{16}$	$5\frac{2}{3}$	$8\frac{1}{4}$	$4\frac{3}{16}$	$2\frac{9}{16}$	$1\frac{1}{6}$	$5\frac{2}{5}$
$\frac{5}{16}$	$1\frac{1}{6}$	$\frac{5}{16}$	$5\frac{2}{5}$	$15\frac{3}{8}$	$4\frac{3}{16}$	$1\frac{1}{6}$	$\frac{5}{16}$	$1\frac{1}{6}$	$5\frac{2}{5}$

■ Tom has $4\frac{2}{3}$ yards of tape. He uses $3\frac{1}{2}$ yards. How much is left?

◸ Lisa worked $3\frac{3}{4}$ hours one day and $4\frac{1}{2}$ hours the next day. Find the total for two days.

◿ A rod is $7\frac{1}{2}$ inches long. A piece $3\frac{5}{16}$ inches long is cut off. How much is left?

◺ Sam has $3\frac{3}{8}$ yards of string. He uses $2\frac{1}{4}$ yards. How much is left?

◺ A carton weighs $\frac{5}{16}$ of a pound. The contents weigh $2\frac{1}{4}$ pounds. What is the total weight?

◺ A roll of wall paper is $9\frac{1}{6}$ yards long. Rita needs only $3\frac{1}{2}$ yards. How much is left?

◸ Two boards are used for a shelf. One board is $5\frac{5}{8}$ inches wide. The other is $9\frac{3}{4}$ inches wide. Find the total width of the shelf.

■ A board is $\frac{3}{4}$ of an inch thick. A nail, $1\frac{1}{16}$ inches long, is driven into the board. How much of the nail will come through on the other side?

■ During a quarter of 15 minutes one team had the ball $9\frac{3}{5}$ minutes. How long did the other team have the ball?

◸ A skirt requires $2\frac{1}{4}$ yards of material. A matching blouse requires $1\frac{3}{8}$ yards. How much material must be bought?

◿ Each morning Mr. James jogs $1\frac{3}{4}$ miles and walks $1\frac{5}{6}$ miles. How far does he jog and walk?

◿ One piece of steak weighs $2\frac{3}{4}$ pounds. Another piece weighs $1\frac{2}{3}$ pounds. What is the total weight?

33 APPLICATIONS

Name ______________________

$10\frac{17}{24}$	$1\frac{19}{32}$	$3\frac{5}{8}$	$1\frac{13}{24}$	$2\frac{3}{8}$	$\frac{19}{32}$	$10\frac{3}{20}$	$5\frac{13}{16}$	$1\frac{3}{8}$	$1\frac{5}{16}$
$\frac{11}{16}$	$5\frac{13}{16}$	$10\frac{17}{24}$	$1\frac{19}{32}$	$3\frac{5}{8}$	$\frac{4}{15}$	$5\frac{13}{15}$	$\frac{7}{10}$	$3\frac{5}{8}$	$1\frac{3}{8}$
$5\frac{13}{16}$	$3\frac{5}{8}$	$\frac{5}{16}$	$\frac{4}{15}$	$\frac{11}{16}$	$5\frac{13}{15}$	$3\frac{5}{8}$	$1\frac{11}{16}$	$\frac{4}{15}$	$5\frac{13}{16}$
$5\frac{13}{16}$	$1\frac{13}{24}$	$9\frac{3}{20}$	$10\frac{3}{20}$	$\frac{4}{15}$	$5\frac{13}{16}$	$10\frac{17}{24}$	$2\frac{3}{8}$	$1\frac{5}{16}$	$3\frac{5}{8}$
$1\frac{13}{24}$	$2\frac{13}{24}$	$1\frac{19}{32}$	$\frac{4}{15}$	$3\frac{5}{8}$	$\frac{4}{15}$	$5\frac{13}{16}$	$1\frac{3}{8}$	$2\frac{5}{8}$	$\frac{7}{10}$
$5\frac{13}{15}$	$10\frac{3}{20}$	$3\frac{5}{8}$	$10\frac{17}{24}$	$5\frac{13}{16}$	$\frac{4}{15}$	$1\frac{5}{16}$	$5\frac{13}{16}$	$1\frac{13}{24}$	$\frac{11}{16}$
$\frac{4}{15}$	$2\frac{5}{8}$	$\frac{5}{16}$	$1\frac{19}{32}$	$3\frac{5}{8}$	$\frac{4}{15}$	$1\frac{3}{8}$	$2\frac{13}{24}$	$9\frac{3}{20}$	$3\frac{5}{8}$
$3\frac{5}{8}$	$1\frac{11}{16}$	$5\frac{13}{16}$	$\frac{4}{15}$	$10\frac{17}{24}$	$\frac{7}{10}$	$5\frac{13}{16}$	$\frac{4}{15}$	$2\frac{3}{8}$	$\frac{4}{15}$
$5\frac{13}{16}$	$2\frac{5}{8}$	$\frac{7}{10}$	$3\frac{5}{8}$	$1\frac{11}{16}$	$\frac{5}{16}$	$5\frac{13}{16}$	$1\frac{13}{24}$	$2\frac{13}{24}$	$\frac{4}{15}$
$5\frac{13}{16}$	$5\frac{13}{15}$	$2\frac{13}{24}$	$2\frac{5}{8}$	$\frac{11}{16}$	$1\frac{3}{8}$	$\frac{19}{32}$	$9\frac{3}{20}$	$1\frac{19}{32}$	$3\frac{5}{8}$

A crew has painted $7\frac{5}{6}$ miles of road. They must paint $9\frac{3}{8}$ miles in all. How much is left?

A stock's price rose $1\frac{3}{4}$ points one day and $1\frac{7}{8}$ the next. Find the total.

Roy runs 100 yards in $10\frac{9}{10}$ seconds. Pete runs it in $11\frac{3}{5}$ seconds. How much faster is Roy?

Kay worked $4\frac{2}{5}$ hours on Friday and $5\frac{3}{4}$ hours on Saturday. How many hours did she work both days?

A rectangle is $3\frac{3}{16}$ inches long and $2\frac{5}{8}$ inches wide. Find the sum of the length and width.

One calculator has a width of $3\frac{3}{8}$ inches. Another has a width of $2\frac{11}{16}$ inches. Find the difference in their widths.

It takes $6\frac{3}{8}$ yards of material to make curtains and $4\frac{1}{3}$ yards to make a matching spread. How much material is needed?

One song on a record plays for $3\frac{2}{3}$ minutes. Another song plays for $2\frac{1}{5}$ minutes. How long does it take to play both songs?

Wilma long-jumped $5\frac{1}{4}$ inches more than the school record. Janie jumped $3\frac{7}{8}$ inches more than the record. How much further did Wilma jump?

One size of scoop for measuring recipes equals $\frac{2}{3}$ of a cup. Another size of scoop equals $\frac{2}{5}$ of a cup. What part of a cup is the difference in their sizes?

A carton for shipping is $10\frac{1}{2}$ inches long, $7\frac{3}{4}$ inches wide, and $6\frac{7}{16}$ inches deep. How much greater is the width than the depth?

Two pieces of metal are to be bolted together. One piece is $\frac{13}{16}$ of an inch thick. The other is $\frac{25}{32}$ of an inch thick. Find the total thickness.

34 MULTIPLICATION

Name _____

$\frac{5}{14}$	$\frac{35}{48}$	$\frac{15}{32}$	$\frac{1}{21}$	$\frac{8}{15}$	$\frac{5}{14}$	$\frac{27}{40}$	$\frac{24}{35}$	$\frac{35}{48}$	$\frac{5}{14}$
$\frac{8}{15}$	$\frac{5}{48}$	$\frac{8}{49}$	$\frac{5}{18}$	$\frac{6}{25}$	$\frac{15}{32}$	$\frac{14}{27}$	$\frac{3}{28}$	$\frac{1}{21}$	$\frac{8}{15}$
$\frac{27}{40}$	$\frac{14}{27}$	$\frac{15}{32}$	$\frac{24}{35}$	$\frac{21}{32}$	$\frac{1}{10}$	$\frac{5}{48}$	$\frac{6}{25}$	$\frac{5}{18}$	$\frac{6}{25}$
$\frac{5}{18}$	$\frac{1}{21}$	$\frac{8}{15}$	$\frac{35}{48}$	$\frac{7}{24}$	$\frac{7}{24}$	$\frac{5}{14}$	$\frac{8}{15}$	$\frac{27}{40}$	$\frac{8}{49}$
$\frac{15}{32}$	$\frac{8}{49}$	$\frac{5}{14}$	$\frac{27}{40}$	$\frac{7}{24}$	$\frac{7}{24}$	$\frac{1}{21}$	$\frac{35}{48}$	$\frac{3}{28}$	$\frac{1}{21}$
$\frac{21}{32}$	$\frac{1}{21}$	$\frac{35}{48}$	$\frac{3}{28}$	$\frac{1}{10}$	$\frac{3}{28}$	$\frac{1}{10}$	$\frac{5}{14}$	$\frac{15}{32}$	$\frac{8}{49}$
$\frac{24}{35}$	$\frac{3}{28}$	$\frac{6}{25}$	$\frac{8}{15}$	$\frac{5}{14}$	$\frac{35}{48}$	$\frac{8}{15}$	$\frac{5}{48}$	$\frac{14}{27}$	$\frac{27}{40}$
$\frac{1}{10}$	$\frac{8}{15}$	$\frac{5}{18}$	$\frac{24}{35}$	$\frac{5}{48}$	$\frac{6}{25}$	$\frac{27}{40}$	$\frac{1}{10}$	$\frac{5}{14}$	$\frac{3}{28}$
$\frac{6}{25}$	$\frac{27}{40}$	$\frac{6}{25}$	$\frac{21}{32}$	$\frac{14}{27}$	$\frac{5}{18}$	$\frac{8}{49}$	$\frac{15}{32}$	$\frac{1}{21}$	$\frac{15}{32}$
$\frac{5}{18}$	$\frac{8}{49}$	$\frac{3}{28}$	$\frac{1}{21}$	$\frac{35}{48}$	$\frac{5}{14}$	$\frac{5}{48}$	$\frac{14}{27}$	$\frac{21}{32}$	$\frac{1}{10}$

■ $\frac{1}{2} \times \frac{5}{7}$

◨ $\frac{3}{4} \times \frac{5}{8}$

◪ $\frac{4}{7} \times \frac{2}{7}$

◿ $\frac{7}{9} \times \frac{2}{3}$ ◺ $\frac{5}{6} \times \frac{1}{3}$ ◤ $\frac{1}{3} \times \frac{1}{7}$ ◿ $\frac{1}{4} \times \frac{5}{12}$

◿ $\frac{1}{2} \times \frac{1}{5}$ ■ $\frac{7}{8} \times \frac{5}{6}$ ◤ $\frac{1}{2} \times \frac{3}{14}$ ◹ $\frac{2}{5} \times \frac{3}{5}$

◺ $\frac{7}{8} \times \frac{3}{4}$ ◹ $\frac{4}{5} \times \frac{6}{7}$ ■ $\frac{2}{3} \times \frac{4}{5}$ ◿ $\frac{3}{4} \times \frac{9}{10}$

Name _____

$\frac{5}{26}$	$\frac{5}{7}$	$\frac{2}{15}$	$\frac{7}{24}$	$\frac{2}{15}$	$\frac{5}{7}$	$\frac{5}{22}$	$\frac{3}{8}$	$\frac{5}{7}$	$\frac{6}{11}$
$\frac{2}{15}$	$\frac{17}{19}$	$\frac{9}{14}$	$\frac{3}{8}$	$\frac{5}{7}$	$\frac{3}{8}$	$\frac{2}{15}$	$\frac{7}{10}$	$\frac{17}{19}$	$\frac{3}{8}$
$\frac{5}{7}$	$\frac{1}{6}$	$\frac{9}{23}$	$\frac{17}{19}$	$\frac{12}{17}$	$\frac{7}{10}$	$\frac{17}{19}$	$\frac{9}{23}$	$\frac{9}{32}$	$\frac{5}{7}$
$\frac{2}{7}$	$\frac{3}{8}$	$\frac{17}{19}$	$\frac{9}{32}$	$\frac{7}{24}$	$\frac{5}{26}$	$\frac{1}{6}$	$\frac{17}{19}$	$\frac{2}{15}$	$\frac{4}{7}$
$\frac{5}{7}$	$\frac{2}{15}$	$\frac{6}{11}$	$\frac{9}{14}$	$\frac{7}{24}$	$\frac{9}{32}$	$\frac{3}{20}$	$\frac{5}{26}$	$\frac{3}{8}$	$\frac{5}{7}$
$\frac{3}{8}$	$\frac{5}{7}$	$\frac{4}{7}$	$\frac{5}{22}$	$\frac{3}{20}$	$\frac{9}{14}$	$\frac{6}{11}$	$\frac{2}{7}$	$\frac{2}{15}$	$\frac{3}{8}$
$\frac{5}{22}$	$\frac{3}{8}$	$\frac{17}{19}$	$\frac{12}{17}$	$\frac{3}{20}$	$\frac{12}{17}$	$\frac{4}{7}$	$\frac{17}{19}$	$\frac{5}{7}$	$\frac{1}{6}$
$\frac{2}{15}$	$\frac{3}{20}$	$\frac{9}{23}$	$\frac{17}{19}$	$\frac{5}{22}$	$\frac{6}{11}$	$\frac{17}{19}$	$\frac{9}{23}$	$\frac{2}{7}$	$\frac{2}{15}$
$\frac{5}{7}$	$\frac{17}{19}$	$\frac{5}{26}$	$\frac{2}{15}$	$\frac{5}{7}$	$\frac{3}{8}$	$\frac{5}{7}$	$\frac{7}{24}$	$\frac{17}{19}$	$\frac{3}{8}$
$\frac{9}{14}$	$\frac{3}{8}$	$\frac{5}{7}$	$\frac{3}{20}$	$\frac{3}{8}$	$\frac{2}{15}$	$\frac{12}{17}$	$\frac{3}{8}$	$\frac{2}{15}$	$\frac{7}{10}$

Reduce each answer if possible.

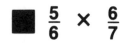 $\frac{5}{6} \times \frac{6}{7}$

◨ $\frac{7}{8} \times \frac{4}{5}$

◨ $\frac{3}{7} \times \frac{21}{32}$

◨ $\frac{6}{11} \times \frac{5}{12}$ ◨ $\frac{7}{9} \times \frac{3}{8}$ ◧ $\frac{9}{10} \times \frac{5}{7}$ ◨ $\frac{9}{10} \times \frac{1}{6}$

◨ $\frac{6}{13} \times \frac{5}{12}$ ■ $\frac{4}{5} \times \frac{1}{6}$ ◨ $\frac{5}{6} \times \frac{1}{5}$ ◧ $\frac{6}{7} \times \frac{14}{17}$

◨ $\frac{2}{3} \times \frac{9}{11}$ ◧ $\frac{6}{7} \times \frac{1}{3}$ ■ $\frac{5}{8} \times \frac{3}{5}$ ◨ $\frac{2}{3} \times \frac{6}{7}$

36 MULTIPLICATION

Name ____________________

11	10	25	8	6	2	14	16	10	11
2	9	50	21	18	9	15	$1\frac{1}{5}$	8	2
50	21	$2\frac{1}{3}$	14	16	32	18	32	16	9
32	18	$1\frac{1}{5}$	15	9	8	21	50	$1\frac{1}{5}$	15
10	11	$2\frac{1}{3}$	2	32	15	6	25	11	6
6	21	18	$1\frac{1}{5}$	8	14	18	14	$2\frac{1}{3}$	10
18	2	25	$2\frac{1}{3}$	21	15	25	16	2	14
5	50	10	9	18	$1\frac{1}{5}$	8	6	9	5
2	11	8	21	15	32	16	$1\frac{1}{5}$	11	10
6	10	5	50	$1\frac{1}{5}$	50	9	5	6	2

Reduce each answer if possible.

■ $6 \times \frac{5}{3}$

◩ $\frac{1}{10} \times 12$

◪ $\frac{5}{7} \times 21$

◪ $\frac{7}{9} \times 3$ ⬕ $\frac{5}{3} \times 15$ ⬔ $\frac{5}{6} \times 60$ ◩ $\frac{7}{8} \times 16$

◪ $22 \times \frac{8}{11}$ ■ $\frac{1}{7} \times 14$ ⬕ $10 \times \frac{16}{5}$ ⬔ $21 \times \frac{6}{7}$

⬕ $\frac{7}{9} \times 27$ ⬔ $56 \times \frac{1}{7}$ ■ $\frac{2}{5} \times 15$ ◩ $24 \times \frac{3}{8}$

Name _____

20	21	36	40	20	40	16	35	36	40
66	16	$4\frac{2}{3}$	60	54	30	66	24	$4\frac{2}{3}$	44
24	35	44	$4\frac{2}{3}$	45	54	20	21	60	40
21	16	$5\frac{2}{3}$	36	30	45	35	16	$5\frac{2}{3}$	60
20	66	44	40	44	66	20	66	36	$4\frac{2}{3}$
60	$4\frac{2}{3}$	20	35	24	$4\frac{2}{3}$	44	40	24	35
$5\frac{2}{3}$	44	66	16	30	54	$4\frac{2}{3}$	44	21	20
36	$4\frac{2}{3}$	20	21	54	45	36	40	16	35
40	36	66	16	45	30	$5\frac{2}{3}$	36	66	20
60	$5\frac{2}{3}$	24	35	44	21	60	$4\frac{2}{3}$	24	21

Reduce each answer if possible.

■ $4\frac{1}{2} \times 12$

◩ $16 \times 2\frac{1}{4}$

◪ $1\frac{1}{9} \times 36$

◪ $4 \times 1\frac{1}{6}$　　◣ $1\frac{1}{9} \times 18$　　◺ $14 \times 2\frac{1}{2}$　　◩ $2\frac{1}{5} \times 20$

◪ $3 \times 1\frac{8}{9}$　　■ $2\frac{1}{7} \times 21$　　◥ $14 \times 1\frac{5}{7}$　　◺ $1\frac{5}{6} \times 36$

◣ $10 \times 1\frac{3}{5}$　　◺ $12 \times 1\frac{3}{4}$　　■ $3\frac{1}{3} \times 9$　　◩ $2\frac{1}{7} \times 28$

Name _____

$2\frac{17}{23}$	$4\frac{2}{5}$	$1\frac{10}{11}$	$1\frac{11}{17}$	$\frac{1}{2}$	$1\frac{10}{11}$	$1\frac{11}{17}$	$\frac{1}{2}$	$1\frac{5}{16}$	$4\frac{2}{5}$
$2\frac{1}{3}$	$2\frac{7}{8}$	$1\frac{1}{3}$	$1\frac{5}{16}$	$\frac{9}{10}$	$2\frac{6}{17}$	$\frac{9}{10}$	$2\frac{17}{23}$	$3\frac{1}{3}$	$2\frac{3}{26}$
$\frac{1}{2}$	$3\frac{3}{10}$	$2\frac{7}{8}$	$2\frac{3}{26}$	$3\frac{3}{10}$	$1\frac{4}{5}$	$1\frac{9}{10}$	$2\frac{7}{8}$	$1\frac{4}{5}$	$1\frac{11}{17}$
$1\frac{11}{17}$	$1\frac{5}{16}$	$1\frac{4}{5}$	$\frac{1}{2}$	$1\frac{1}{3}$	$1\frac{5}{16}$	$1\frac{10}{11}$	$3\frac{3}{10}$	$\frac{9}{10}$	$\frac{1}{2}$
$1\frac{10}{11}$	$1\frac{9}{10}$	$1\frac{1}{3}$	$2\frac{1}{3}$	$2\frac{7}{8}$	$3\frac{1}{3}$	$1\frac{4}{5}$	$2\frac{6}{17}$	$1\frac{11}{13}$	$1\frac{10}{11}$
$\frac{1}{2}$	$2\frac{6}{17}$	$1\frac{11}{13}$	$2\frac{17}{23}$	$3\frac{1}{3}$	$2\frac{7}{8}$	$\frac{9}{10}$	$2\frac{1}{3}$	$1\frac{1}{3}$	$1\frac{11}{17}$
$1\frac{11}{17}$	$3\frac{3}{10}$	$\frac{9}{10}$	$1\frac{11}{17}$	$1\frac{11}{13}$	$3\frac{3}{10}$	$\frac{1}{2}$	$2\frac{17}{23}$	$1\frac{4}{5}$	$\frac{1}{2}$
$\frac{1}{2}$	$2\frac{17}{23}$	$2\frac{7}{8}$	$4\frac{2}{5}$	$2\frac{6}{17}$	$4\frac{2}{5}$	$1\frac{5}{16}$	$2\frac{7}{8}$	$4\frac{2}{5}$	$1\frac{10}{11}$
$1\frac{5}{16}$	$3\frac{1}{3}$	$2\frac{3}{26}$	$3\frac{3}{10}$	$1\frac{11}{13}$	$2\frac{1}{3}$	$1\frac{4}{5}$	$1\frac{9}{10}$	$3\frac{1}{3}$	$4\frac{2}{5}$
$2\frac{1}{3}$	$1\frac{4}{5}$	$1\frac{10}{11}$	$1\frac{11}{17}$	$\frac{1}{2}$	$1\frac{10}{11}$	$\frac{1}{2}$	$1\frac{11}{17}$	$3\frac{3}{10}$	$2\frac{3}{26}$

Reduce each answer if possible.

■ $1\frac{1}{2} \times \frac{1}{3}$

◪ $5\frac{1}{4} \times \frac{12}{23}$

◪ $\frac{9}{13} \times 2\frac{2}{3}$

◪ $4\frac{1}{2} \times \frac{2}{5}$ ◪ $\frac{9}{10} \times 3\frac{2}{3}$ ◹ $5\frac{1}{2} \times \frac{4}{5}$ ◪ $1\frac{2}{5} \times \frac{15}{16}$

◪ $2\frac{3}{4} \times \frac{10}{13}$ ■ $1\frac{3}{4} \times \frac{16}{17}$ ◨ $\frac{7}{10} \times 2\frac{5}{7}$ ◹ $3\frac{1}{3} \times \frac{2}{5}$

◺ $4\frac{2}{3} \times \frac{1}{2}$ ◹ $\frac{3}{7} \times 2\frac{1}{10}$ ■ $2\frac{1}{3} \times \frac{9}{11}$ ◪ $2\frac{2}{3} \times \frac{15}{17}$

39 MULTIPLICATION

Name _____

$3\frac{1}{5}$	$5\frac{1}{4}$	$4\frac{4}{5}$	12	18	6	8	$5\frac{1}{4}$	$3\frac{1}{5}$	$4\frac{4}{5}$
$4\frac{4}{5}$	3	4	$5\frac{1}{4}$	14	24	$3\frac{1}{5}$	$2\frac{2}{5}$	32	$5\frac{1}{4}$
$5\frac{1}{4}$	$2\frac{2}{5}$	45	$3\frac{1}{5}$	$4\frac{4}{5}$	$5\frac{1}{4}$	$4\frac{4}{5}$	$3\frac{1}{2}$	8	$3\frac{1}{5}$
$3\frac{1}{5}$	6	$2\frac{3}{4}$	18	$5\frac{1}{4}$	$3\frac{1}{5}$	3	$9\frac{7}{8}$	45	$4\frac{4}{5}$
18	14	$9\frac{7}{8}$	8	$3\frac{1}{2}$	45	12	$2\frac{3}{4}$	4	3
$2\frac{2}{5}$	32	$5\frac{1}{4}$	$3\frac{1}{5}$	$4\frac{4}{5}$	$5\frac{1}{4}$	$4\frac{4}{5}$	$3\frac{1}{5}$	6	24
$5\frac{1}{4}$	14	45	6	32	3	18	$3\frac{1}{2}$	4	$5\frac{1}{4}$
$3\frac{1}{5}$	$4\frac{4}{5}$	12	24	14	4	12	8	$3\frac{1}{5}$	$4\frac{4}{5}$
$3\frac{1}{2}$	18	$3\frac{1}{5}$	6	32	3	45	$4\frac{4}{5}$	$3\frac{1}{2}$	18
24	$2\frac{2}{5}$	$2\frac{3}{4}$	4	14	8	12	$2\frac{3}{4}$	24	$2\frac{2}{5}$

Reduce each answer if possible.

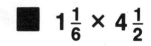 $1\frac{1}{6} \times 4\frac{1}{2}$

◪ $2\frac{1}{3} \times 1\frac{1}{2}$

◣ $2\frac{2}{5} \times 1\frac{2}{3}$

◪ $3\frac{1}{3} \times 2\frac{2}{5}$ ◸ $2\frac{1}{4} \times 1\frac{1}{15}$ ◹ $3\frac{3}{4} \times 4\frac{4}{5}$ ◪ $2\frac{1}{4} \times 2\frac{2}{3}$

◧ $2\frac{5}{8} \times 9\frac{1}{7}$ ■ $2\frac{2}{3} \times 1\frac{1}{5}$ ◹ $3\frac{9}{11} \times 3\frac{2}{3}$ ◺ $9\frac{1}{7} \times 3\frac{1}{2}$

◺ $2\frac{1}{3} \times 5\frac{1}{7}$ ◹ $40\frac{1}{2} \times 1\frac{1}{9}$ ■ $1\frac{1}{11} \times 4\frac{2}{5}$ ◪ $1\frac{1}{7} \times 2\frac{5}{8}$

Name _____

$\frac{1}{42}$	$\frac{15}{28}$	2	$4\frac{1}{2}$	5	$8\frac{1}{4}$	28	6	$\frac{1}{2}$	$\frac{15}{28}$
$\frac{1}{2}$	20	12	$2\frac{1}{2}$	25	$11\frac{1}{3}$	$1\frac{1}{6}$	20	12	$\frac{1}{42}$
$1\frac{1}{6}$	28	6	2	$1\frac{1}{6}$	$2\frac{1}{2}$	$4\frac{1}{2}$	28	6	$11\frac{1}{3}$
$4\frac{1}{2}$	$11\frac{1}{3}$	25	$\frac{1}{2}$	5	$8\frac{1}{4}$	$\frac{1}{42}$	$2\frac{1}{2}$	25	28
12	5	28	12	$\frac{15}{28}$	$\frac{1}{2}$	20	6	$4\frac{1}{2}$	20
$8\frac{1}{4}$	$2\frac{1}{2}$	$2\frac{1}{2}$	$8\frac{1}{4}$	$\frac{1}{2}$	$\frac{1}{42}$	28	$1\frac{1}{6}$	12	2
$1\frac{1}{6}$	2	$4\frac{1}{2}$	$\frac{15}{28}$	$11\frac{1}{3}$	$1\frac{1}{6}$	$\frac{1}{2}$	2	6	$2\frac{1}{2}$
6	20	25	$2\frac{1}{2}$	6	5	25	20	$1\frac{1}{6}$	5
$\frac{1}{42}$	28	$4\frac{1}{2}$	2	$8\frac{1}{4}$	5	6	28	$4\frac{1}{2}$	$\frac{15}{28}$
$\frac{1}{2}$	$\frac{15}{28}$	$2\frac{1}{2}$	$1\frac{1}{6}$	20	12	$11\frac{1}{3}$	25	$\frac{15}{28}$	$\frac{1}{42}$

Reduce each answer if possible.

■ $\dfrac{5}{7} \times \dfrac{3}{4}$

◩ $\dfrac{15}{2} \times \dfrac{8}{3}$

◪ $6\dfrac{2}{3} \times \dfrac{9}{10}$

◪ $3\dfrac{2}{3} \times 2\dfrac{1}{4}$ ◣ $6 \times \dfrac{1}{3}$ ◨ $4\dfrac{1}{2} \times 2\dfrac{2}{3}$ ◪ $\dfrac{17}{8} \times \dfrac{16}{3}$

◪ $2\dfrac{1}{5} \times 2\dfrac{1}{22}$ ■ $\dfrac{2}{3} \times \dfrac{3}{4}$ ◤ $6\dfrac{2}{3} \times 4\dfrac{1}{5}$ ◿ $\dfrac{7}{8} \times 1\dfrac{1}{3}$

◣ $20 \times \dfrac{1}{4}$ ◸ $6\dfrac{2}{3} \times 3\dfrac{3}{4}$ ■ $\dfrac{1}{6} \times \dfrac{1}{7}$ ◪ $\dfrac{15}{4} \times \dfrac{2}{3}$

Name _____

9	$1\frac{1}{11}$	$1\frac{1}{6}$	$1\frac{1}{2}$	$\frac{4}{5}$	1	$2\frac{1}{2}$	1	$1\frac{1}{6}$	$\frac{2}{3}$
$\frac{1}{3}$	$\frac{5}{6}$	2	$\frac{4}{5}$	$1\frac{1}{3}$	3	$1\frac{1}{11}$	$\frac{5}{6}$	2	$2\frac{1}{4}$
$1\frac{1}{2}$	$1\frac{1}{6}$	1	3	$\frac{3}{4}$	$\frac{2}{3}$	$1\frac{1}{2}$	$2\frac{1}{4}$	$1\frac{1}{11}$	$2\frac{1}{2}$
$\frac{3}{4}$	2	$2\frac{1}{2}$	9	1	$\frac{4}{5}$	$\frac{3}{4}$	$1\frac{1}{3}$	3	9
$2\frac{1}{4}$	9	$\frac{2}{3}$	$\frac{3}{4}$	9	$\frac{2}{3}$	9	$\frac{2}{3}$	$\frac{3}{4}$	$\frac{1}{3}$
$1\frac{1}{3}$	$\frac{4}{5}$	$\frac{3}{4}$	1	$\frac{4}{5}$	$1\frac{1}{11}$	$1\frac{1}{6}$	9	$1\frac{1}{11}$	3
$\frac{1}{3}$	$\frac{5}{6}$	$\frac{1}{3}$	$\frac{5}{6}$	$1\frac{1}{2}$	3	$1\frac{1}{3}$	$2\frac{1}{4}$	$1\frac{1}{2}$	$\frac{4}{5}$
3	9	$1\frac{1}{3}$	$2\frac{1}{4}$	1	$\frac{4}{5}$	$\frac{1}{3}$	$\frac{5}{6}$	$\frac{2}{3}$	2
$1\frac{1}{6}$	$\frac{3}{4}$	$\frac{2}{3}$	2	3	2	$2\frac{1}{2}$	9	$\frac{3}{4}$	1
2	$\frac{4}{5}$	9	$\frac{3}{4}$	$1\frac{1}{11}$	$1\frac{1}{6}$	$\frac{2}{3}$	$\frac{3}{4}$	$\frac{1}{3}$	$2\frac{1}{2}$

Reduce each answer if possible.

■ $\frac{4}{9} \div \frac{2}{3}$

◨ $\frac{9}{10} \div \frac{9}{10}$

◨ $\frac{5}{9} \div \frac{2}{9}$

◨ $\frac{5}{7} \div \frac{5}{21}$ ◨ $\frac{3}{4} \div \frac{1}{2}$ ◨ $\frac{7}{8} \div \frac{3}{4}$ ◨ $\frac{3}{4} \div \frac{11}{16}$

◨ $\frac{5}{8} \div \frac{3}{4}$ ■ $\frac{1}{4} \div \frac{1}{3}$ ◨ $\frac{8}{15} \div \frac{2}{5}$ ◨ $\frac{3}{8} \div \frac{1}{6}$

◨ $\frac{7}{11} \div \frac{7}{22}$ ◨ $\frac{2}{3} \div \frac{5}{6}$ ■ $\frac{3}{5} \div \frac{1}{15}$ ◨ $\frac{4}{21} \div \frac{4}{7}$

42 DIVISION

19	10	36	12	10	90	30	18	28	19
33	35	14	16	27	14	16	27	30	42
30	42	12	19	40	18	19	36	33	12
28	14	19	48	42	48	90	19	16	48
40	16	42	30	14	16	35	33	14	35
33	27	12	10	27	14	28	36	27	42
18	14	19	36	18	40	12	19	16	30
10	35	28	19	33	42	19	10	40	28
30	42	16	27	14	16	27	14	10	35
19	36	48	90	30	12	48	42	18	19

Reduce each answer if possible.

■ $12 \div \frac{4}{9}$

◩ $9 \div \frac{3}{4}$

◩ $5 \div \frac{1}{2}$

◩ $21 \div \frac{7}{11}$ ◪ $21 \div \frac{3}{4}$ ◹ $18 \div \frac{3}{5}$ ◩ $15 \div \frac{3}{7}$

◩ $40 \div \frac{5}{6}$ ■ $10 \div \frac{5}{8}$ ◺ $81 \div \frac{9}{10}$ ◹ $32 \div \frac{4}{5}$

◺ $36 \div \frac{6}{7}$ ◹ $9 \div \frac{1}{4}$ ■ $6 \div \frac{3}{7}$ ◩ $16 \div \frac{8}{9}$

43 DIVISION

10	5	6	$15\frac{1}{2}$	$9\frac{2}{3}$	$1\frac{3}{4}$	$7\frac{1}{2}$	8	5	24
6	8	14	$8\frac{3}{4}$	$3\frac{4}{5}$	$1\frac{3}{4}$	$12\frac{2}{3}$	$1\frac{7}{8}$	6	8
5	24	$7\frac{1}{2}$	14	$1\frac{3}{4}$	$9\frac{2}{3}$	4	$15\frac{1}{2}$	$12\frac{2}{3}$	5
6	8	$3\frac{3}{5}$	$9\frac{2}{3}$	$3\frac{1}{2}$	$8\frac{3}{4}$	$3\frac{4}{5}$	$3\frac{1}{2}$	8	6
$1\frac{7}{8}$	5	6	$3\frac{4}{5}$	10	24	$1\frac{3}{4}$	8	5	$5\frac{2}{3}$
$3\frac{1}{2}$	$5\frac{2}{3}$	$1\frac{7}{8}$	24	$1\frac{7}{8}$	$15\frac{1}{2}$	$12\frac{2}{3}$	14	$7\frac{1}{2}$	$8\frac{3}{4}$
4	24	$12\frac{2}{3}$	$15\frac{1}{2}$	$9\frac{2}{3}$	$1\frac{3}{4}$	4	24	$12\frac{2}{3}$	$15\frac{1}{2}$
$12\frac{2}{3}$	14	$7\frac{1}{2}$	$8\frac{3}{4}$	$3\frac{4}{5}$	$9\frac{2}{3}$	$12\frac{2}{3}$	$5\frac{2}{3}$	4	$3\frac{3}{5}$
$1\frac{7}{8}$	$3\frac{3}{5}$	10	$15\frac{1}{2}$	$1\frac{3}{4}$	$1\frac{3}{4}$	$1\frac{7}{8}$	$3\frac{3}{5}$	$3\frac{1}{2}$	$5\frac{2}{3}$
10	8	5	$8\frac{3}{4}$	$9\frac{2}{3}$	$3\frac{4}{5}$	10	6	5	$8\frac{3}{4}$

Reduce each answer if possible.

■ $1\frac{4}{5} \div \frac{3}{10}$

◪ $3\frac{7}{8} \div \frac{1}{4}$

◪ $3\frac{4}{5} \div \frac{3}{10}$

◪ $2\frac{5}{8} \div \frac{3}{4}$ ◪ $1\frac{1}{8} \div \frac{5}{16}$ ◪ $1\frac{1}{4} \div \frac{2}{3}$ ◪ $3\frac{1}{2} \div \frac{1}{4}$

◪ $6\frac{3}{7} \div \frac{9}{14}$ ■ $6\frac{2}{5} \div \frac{4}{5}$ ◪ $5\frac{1}{7} \div \frac{3}{14}$ ◪ $4\frac{1}{2} \div \frac{3}{5}$

◪ $6\frac{1}{8} \div \frac{7}{10}$ ◪ $3\frac{1}{7} \div \frac{11}{14}$ ■ $2\frac{1}{7} \div \frac{3}{7}$ ◪ $4\frac{1}{4} \div \frac{3}{4}$

44 DIVISION

Name _____

$\frac{3}{10}$	$\frac{1}{16}$	$1\frac{5}{7}$	$\frac{1}{4}$	24	$\frac{3}{10}$	6	$\frac{3}{5}$	$\frac{1}{16}$	$\frac{1}{6}$
$\frac{1}{16}$	$\frac{8}{23}$	$1\frac{1}{9}$	$\frac{8}{23}$	$\frac{2}{7}$	$\frac{1}{24}$	$\frac{8}{23}$	$3\frac{10}{13}$	$1\frac{5}{7}$	$\frac{1}{16}$
$\frac{3}{5}$	$\frac{2}{15}$	6	$\frac{3}{5}$	24	$\frac{2}{15}$	$1\frac{5}{7}$	$\frac{5}{12}$	$\frac{1}{6}$	$\frac{8}{23}$
$\frac{1}{6}$	$1\frac{5}{7}$	$\frac{8}{23}$	$1\frac{5}{7}$	$\frac{5}{12}$	6	$\frac{3}{5}$	$\frac{8}{23}$	$1\frac{5}{7}$	$\frac{3}{10}$
$\frac{1}{4}$	6	$\frac{1}{24}$	24	$\frac{3}{5}$	$\frac{8}{23}$	$1\frac{1}{9}$	$\frac{1}{14}$	$\frac{1}{24}$	6
$\frac{2}{15}$	$3\frac{10}{13}$	$1\frac{1}{9}$	$\frac{1}{14}$	$\frac{8}{23}$	$1\frac{5}{7}$	$\frac{1}{24}$	$\frac{1}{6}$	$\frac{2}{15}$	$3\frac{10}{13}$
$\frac{2}{7}$	$\frac{8}{23}$	$1\frac{5}{7}$	$\frac{3}{5}$	$\frac{2}{15}$	$3\frac{10}{13}$	$\frac{3}{5}$	$1\frac{5}{7}$	$\frac{8}{23}$	$\frac{1}{24}$
$1\frac{5}{7}$	$\frac{1}{4}$	$\frac{1}{6}$	$\frac{8}{23}$	$\frac{2}{7}$	$\frac{5}{12}$	$\frac{8}{23}$	$1\frac{1}{9}$	$\frac{1}{14}$	$\frac{3}{5}$
$\frac{1}{16}$	$\frac{8}{23}$	$\frac{5}{12}$	$1\frac{5}{7}$	24	$1\frac{1}{9}$	$\frac{3}{5}$	$\frac{2}{7}$	$\frac{8}{23}$	$\frac{1}{16}$
$\frac{1}{24}$	$\frac{1}{16}$	$\frac{3}{5}$	$\frac{2}{15}$	6	$\frac{1}{4}$	$\frac{1}{6}$	$1\frac{5}{7}$	$\frac{1}{16}$	$\frac{2}{7}$

Reduce each answer if possible.

■ $6 \div 3\frac{1}{2}$

◰ $\frac{3}{8} \div 1\frac{1}{4}$

◨ $16 \div 2\frac{2}{3}$

◰ $\frac{3}{4} \div 2\frac{5}{8}$ ◺ $\frac{7}{8} \div 3\frac{1}{2}$ ◸ $14 \div 3\frac{5}{7}$ ◰ $\frac{4}{9} \div 3\frac{1}{3}$

◰ $\frac{5}{6} \div 11\frac{2}{3}$ ■ $\frac{2}{3} \div 1\frac{1}{9}$ ◺ $\frac{4}{15} \div 6\frac{2}{5}$ ◺ $\frac{9}{16} \div 3\frac{3}{8}$

◺ $\frac{5}{9} \div 1\frac{1}{3}$ ◸ $28 \div 1\frac{1}{6}$ ■ $\frac{4}{5} \div 2\frac{3}{10}$ ◰ $9 \div 8\frac{1}{10}$

45 DIVISION

$\frac{5}{8}$	$\frac{4}{11}$	$1\frac{1}{3}$	$\frac{2}{5}$	$\frac{2}{7}$	$\frac{1}{10}$	$\frac{2}{3}$	$\frac{7}{8}$	$\frac{4}{7}$	$1\frac{1}{7}$
$\frac{3}{5}$	$\frac{3}{4}$	$\frac{1}{10}$	$\frac{2}{7}$	$\frac{2}{5}$	$\frac{2}{3}$	$1\frac{1}{7}$	$\frac{4}{7}$	$1\frac{1}{2}$	$\frac{3}{7}$
$1\frac{1}{7}$	$\frac{2}{3}$	$\frac{3}{8}$	$1\frac{1}{2}$	$\frac{4}{7}$	$\frac{1}{10}$	$\frac{3}{4}$	$\frac{3}{8}$	$\frac{7}{8}$	$\frac{4}{7}$
$\frac{3}{7}$	$\frac{2}{7}$	$\frac{3}{4}$	$\frac{3}{8}$	$\frac{2}{3}$	$\frac{7}{8}$	$\frac{3}{8}$	$1\frac{1}{2}$	$1\frac{1}{7}$	$1\frac{1}{3}$
$\frac{4}{7}$	$\frac{2}{5}$	$\frac{5}{8}$	$\frac{4}{11}$	$\frac{1}{8}$	$\frac{1}{7}$	$\frac{4}{7}$	$\frac{1}{10}$	$1\frac{1}{3}$	$\frac{1}{10}$
$\frac{3}{5}$	$\frac{1}{10}$	$\frac{3}{5}$	$\frac{2}{5}$	$\frac{1}{8}$	$\frac{1}{7}$	$\frac{3}{5}$	$\frac{3}{7}$	$\frac{2}{7}$	$\frac{3}{7}$
$1\frac{1}{7}$	$1\frac{1}{3}$	$1\frac{1}{2}$	$\frac{3}{4}$	$\frac{5}{8}$	$\frac{4}{11}$	$\frac{3}{8}$	$1\frac{1}{2}$	$\frac{7}{8}$	$\frac{4}{7}$
$\frac{3}{7}$	$\frac{2}{7}$	$\frac{3}{4}$	$\frac{3}{8}$	$1\frac{1}{3}$	$\frac{3}{7}$	$1\frac{1}{2}$	$\frac{3}{4}$	$\frac{4}{11}$	$\frac{3}{5}$
$\frac{5}{8}$	$\frac{3}{4}$	$\frac{2}{5}$	$\frac{2}{3}$	$\frac{4}{11}$	$\frac{5}{8}$	$\frac{7}{8}$	$1\frac{1}{3}$	$1\frac{1}{2}$	$1\frac{1}{7}$
$\frac{3}{5}$	$\frac{7}{8}$	$\frac{5}{8}$	$\frac{1}{10}$	$1\frac{1}{3}$	$\frac{2}{5}$	$\frac{2}{7}$	$\frac{4}{11}$	$\frac{2}{3}$	$\frac{3}{7}$

Reduce each answer if possible.

■ $10\frac{1}{2} \div 7$

◩ $2\frac{5}{8} \div 3$

◪ $1\frac{5}{7} \div 6$

◪ $3\frac{1}{8} \div 5$ ◨ $5\frac{5}{11} \div 15$ ◩ $9\frac{1}{3} \div 14$ ◪ $4\frac{4}{5} \div 12$

◨ $5\frac{1}{7} \div 9$ ■ $3\frac{3}{4} \div 5$ ◩ $3\frac{2}{5} \div 34$ ◧ $5\frac{1}{3} \div 4$

◨ $10\frac{2}{7} \div 9$ ◪ $6\frac{3}{5} \div 11$ ■ $3\frac{3}{8} \div 9$ ◪ $4\frac{2}{7} \div 10$

Name _____

$1\frac{5}{7}$	4	$2\frac{1}{4}$	$\frac{3}{4}$	$\frac{3}{5}$	4	$4\frac{4}{5}$	$2\frac{1}{7}$	$1\frac{1}{2}$	$7\frac{4}{11}$
$1\frac{3}{5}$	$9\frac{1}{4}$	$8\frac{5}{8}$	$1\frac{5}{7}$	$\frac{5}{7}$	$9\frac{1}{4}$	$1\frac{5}{7}$	$4\frac{4}{5}$	$\frac{5}{7}$	$2\frac{1}{4}$
$\frac{3}{4}$	$2\frac{1}{4}$	$7\frac{4}{11}$	$1\frac{7}{9}$	$1\frac{12}{13}$	$\frac{2}{3}$	$1\frac{7}{9}$	$7\frac{4}{11}$	4	6
$1\frac{1}{2}$	$7\frac{4}{11}$	$1\frac{5}{7}$	$7\frac{4}{11}$	$1\frac{1}{2}$	$1\frac{3}{5}$	$1\frac{5}{7}$	$1\frac{7}{9}$	$1\frac{5}{7}$	$1\frac{3}{5}$
6	$1\frac{7}{9}$	$7\frac{4}{11}$	$8\frac{5}{8}$	$9\frac{1}{4}$	$3\frac{1}{3}$	$\frac{2}{3}$	$7\frac{4}{11}$	$1\frac{7}{9}$	$1\frac{12}{13}$
$7\frac{4}{11}$	$2\frac{1}{7}$	6	4	$3\frac{1}{3}$	$\frac{5}{7}$	$\frac{3}{5}$	$1\frac{12}{13}$	$2\frac{1}{4}$	$1\frac{5}{7}$
$1\frac{7}{9}$	$3\frac{1}{3}$	$1\frac{5}{7}$	$7\frac{4}{11}$	$4\frac{4}{5}$	$8\frac{5}{8}$	$7\frac{4}{11}$	$1\frac{7}{9}$	$3\frac{1}{3}$	$7\frac{4}{11}$
$2\frac{1}{4}$	$1\frac{12}{13}$	$9\frac{1}{4}$	$1\frac{7}{9}$	4	$\frac{3}{5}$	$1\frac{5}{7}$	$9\frac{1}{4}$	$\frac{2}{3}$	4
$8\frac{5}{8}$	$\frac{3}{5}$	$\frac{3}{4}$	$\frac{5}{7}$	6	$\frac{3}{4}$	$3\frac{1}{3}$	6	$1\frac{3}{5}$	$4\frac{4}{5}$
$7\frac{4}{11}$	$\frac{3}{4}$	$1\frac{1}{2}$	$7\frac{4}{11}$	4	$2\frac{1}{4}$	$1\frac{7}{9}$	$2\frac{1}{7}$	6	$1\frac{7}{9}$

Reduce each answer if possible.

■ $3\frac{3}{7} \div 1\frac{13}{14}$

◩ $7\frac{1}{3} \div 1\frac{5}{6}$

◩ $8\frac{2}{5} \div 1\frac{2}{5}$

◩ $5\frac{1}{3} \div 1\frac{1}{9}$　　◩ $9\frac{1}{5} \div 1\frac{1}{15}$　　◺ $2\frac{1}{4} \div 3\frac{3}{4}$　　◩ $4\frac{2}{3} \div 2\frac{11}{12}$

◩ $1\frac{1}{21} \div 1\frac{4}{7}$　　■ $3\frac{3}{4} \div 2\frac{3}{16}$　　◪ $6\frac{1}{4} \div 3\frac{1}{4}$　　◺ $5\frac{1}{16} \div 2\frac{1}{4}$

◪ $1\frac{5}{7} \div 2\frac{2}{7}$　　◺ $5\frac{1}{4} \div 3\frac{1}{2}$　　■ $10\frac{4}{5} \div 1\frac{7}{15}$　　◩ $2\frac{6}{7} \div 1\frac{1}{3}$

47 REVIEW

Name ______________________

1	$\frac{4}{21}$	10	$1\frac{3}{5}$	4	$1\frac{5}{9}$	$6\frac{2}{3}$	$1\frac{1}{2}$	$\frac{4}{21}$	$\frac{4}{9}$
4	$\frac{1}{12}$	8	$\frac{2}{21}$	5	$\frac{1}{12}$	1	$\frac{2}{21}$	5	$1\frac{5}{9}$
$6\frac{2}{3}$	$5\frac{5}{9}$	$\frac{1}{12}$	$1\frac{1}{2}$	$\frac{4}{9}$	$5\frac{5}{9}$	$6\frac{2}{3}$	$1\frac{3}{5}$	6	$1\frac{3}{5}$
$\frac{2}{21}$	$1\frac{3}{5}$	$\frac{4}{9}$	$\frac{7}{8}$	5	$\frac{1}{12}$	$\frac{7}{8}$	8	$\frac{1}{12}$	8
$1\frac{5}{9}$	6	5	6	1	6	$5\frac{5}{9}$	$6\frac{2}{3}$	1	$\frac{4}{21}$
4	10	1	$6\frac{2}{3}$	$1\frac{1}{2}$	10	$1\frac{3}{5}$	$\frac{2}{21}$	5	$1\frac{5}{9}$
$6\frac{2}{3}$	8	10	$\frac{7}{8}$	8	6	$\frac{7}{8}$	$1\frac{1}{2}$	$\frac{4}{9}$	$1\frac{1}{2}$
6	$1\frac{1}{2}$	$\frac{4}{9}$	$5\frac{5}{9}$	$\frac{1}{12}$	5	$\frac{2}{21}$	1	10	1
$\frac{4}{21}$	$\frac{2}{21}$	5	$6\frac{2}{3}$	8	$\frac{4}{9}$	$1\frac{3}{5}$	$\frac{1}{12}$	8	4
$1\frac{3}{5}$	4	$\frac{4}{9}$	$5\frac{5}{9}$	$1\frac{5}{9}$	4	6	$5\frac{5}{9}$	$\frac{4}{21}$	$\frac{1}{12}$

Reduce each answer if possible.

■ $3\frac{1}{2} \div 2\frac{1}{4}$

◤ $25 \div 2\frac{1}{2}$

◢ $4 \div \frac{1}{2}$

◢ $\frac{7}{11} \div \frac{7}{11}$

◣ $\frac{2}{3} \div \frac{3}{2}$

◥ $3\frac{1}{3} \div \frac{2}{3}$

◤ $1\frac{1}{3} \div 16$

◢ $6\frac{2}{3} \div 1\frac{1}{5}$

■ $\frac{6}{7} \div \frac{3}{14}$

◥ $\frac{2}{15} \div 1\frac{2}{5}$

◥ $5\frac{1}{4} \div 3\frac{1}{2}$

◣ $2\frac{4}{5} \div \frac{7}{15}$

◥ $\frac{4}{7} \div \frac{5}{14}$

■ $\frac{1}{7} \div \frac{3}{4}$

◤ $16\frac{2}{3} \div 2\frac{1}{2}$

Name _____

805	14	4	$1\frac{7}{8}$	36	$\frac{7}{16}$	$1\frac{1}{8}$	195	3	$4\frac{2}{3}$
$11\frac{1}{4}$	36	$11\frac{1}{4}$	805	$11\frac{1}{4}$	$1\frac{1}{8}$	195	3	$4\frac{2}{3}$	34
4	$2\frac{1}{8}$	$\frac{7}{16}$	$1\frac{1}{8}$	$4\frac{2}{3}$	805	14	36	$2\frac{1}{8}$	$4\frac{2}{3}$
$1\frac{4}{5}$	$1\frac{7}{8}$	3	$\frac{7}{16}$	34	14	805	$1\frac{7}{8}$	34	$2\frac{1}{8}$
$1\frac{7}{8}$	36	$\frac{7}{16}$	3	195	805	$11\frac{1}{4}$	4	$\frac{7}{16}$	3
195	$1\frac{1}{8}$	14	36	$11\frac{1}{4}$	3	$4\frac{2}{3}$	34	$1\frac{7}{8}$	4
$1\frac{4}{5}$	$4\frac{2}{3}$	4	14	805	$\frac{7}{16}$	$1\frac{1}{8}$	$4\frac{2}{3}$	36	$1\frac{4}{5}$
3	$2\frac{1}{8}$	14	805	$11\frac{1}{4}$	$1\frac{1}{8}$	195	34	$1\frac{4}{5}$	$11\frac{1}{4}$
195	34	$\frac{7}{16}$	3	195	36	14	4	$1\frac{7}{8}$	4
34	195	$1\frac{1}{8}$	$\frac{7}{16}$	$1\frac{1}{8}$	$1\frac{7}{8}$	805	14	36	$1\frac{7}{8}$

One cup of celery seed weighs $2\frac{2}{3}$ oz. How many ounces are in $1\frac{3}{4}$ cups?

A photo is $2\frac{1}{4}$ inches long. It is to be enlarged $1\frac{1}{3}$ times. How long is the enlarged photo?

A can of baked beans holds $1\frac{3}{4}$ cups. What part of a cup is in each of 4 servings?

A mail sack contains 104 flyers. Each weighs $1\frac{7}{8}$ ounces. Find the total weight in ounces.

An artist wants to draw columns on a page $8\frac{1}{2}$ inches wide. Each column is $\frac{1}{4}$ of an inch wide. How many columns can be drawn?

A recipe calls for $\frac{3}{8}$ of a teaspoon of pepper. Sally wants to make three times as much as the recipe calls for. How much pepper will she need?

If $3\frac{1}{2}$ yards of material are needed to make a dress, how many dresses can be made from 49 yards of material?

A plane traveled 460 miles in one hour. At that rate, how many miles can it travel in $1\frac{3}{4}$ hours?

A board 9 inches long is to be cut into pieces $2\frac{1}{4}$ inches long. How many pieces are there?

One inch equals about $2\frac{1}{2}$ centimeters. How many centimeters are there in $4\frac{1}{2}$ inches?

An insect spray requires $\frac{5}{8}$ of an ounce of chemical for one gallon of water. How much is needed for three gallons of water?

A carton of calculators weighed $11\frac{1}{4}$ pounds. The weight of each calculator was $\frac{5}{16}$ of a pound. How many calculators were there?

SOLUTION KEY

1 FRACTIONS

$\frac{4}{6}$ $\frac{2}{4}$ $\frac{2}{10}$

$\frac{1}{4}$ $\frac{6}{12}$ $\frac{5}{6}$ $\frac{1}{3}$

$\frac{3}{4}$ $\frac{5}{8}$ $\frac{4}{5}$ $\frac{3}{8}$

$\frac{2}{6}$ $\frac{1}{6}$ $\frac{7}{8}$ $\frac{2}{5}$

2 REDUCING FRACTIONS

$\frac{3}{4}$ $\frac{2}{8}$ $\frac{4}{2}$

$\frac{7}{12}$ $\frac{7}{4}$ $\frac{7}{8}$ $\frac{5}{7}$

$\frac{5}{6}$ $\frac{4}{3}$ $\frac{5}{9}$ $\frac{1}{2}$

$\frac{7}{16}$ $\frac{3}{3}$ $\frac{2}{7}$ $\frac{1}{6}$

3 IMPROPER FRACTIONS

$3\frac{3}{4}$ $1\frac{5}{6}$ $6\frac{2}{3}$

$2\frac{3}{8}$ $3\frac{4}{7}$ $7\frac{1}{3}$ $3\frac{5}{7}$

$8\frac{1}{7}$ $6\frac{1}{2}$ $6\frac{3}{4}$ $6\frac{5}{7}$

$5\frac{1}{4}$ $5\frac{4}{7}$ $2\frac{1}{4}$ $7\frac{4}{7}$

4 IMPROPER FRACTIONS

$3\frac{1}{4}$ $4\frac{1}{2}$ $3\frac{3}{8}$

$3\frac{5}{6}$ $2\frac{2}{5}$ $2\frac{1}{3}$ $2\frac{1}{2}$

$2\frac{4}{3}$ $3\frac{1}{3}$ $1\frac{7}{8}$ $8\frac{1}{2}$

$2\frac{4}{7}$ $3\frac{3}{5}$ $1\frac{3}{4}$ $1\frac{1}{4}$

5 DECIMALS

$\frac{7}{5}$ $\frac{3}{25}$ $\frac{3}{20}$

$\frac{3}{250}$ $3\frac{31}{100}$ $3\frac{4}{5}$ $\frac{7}{25}$

$2\frac{1}{50}$ $2\frac{1}{2}$ $1\frac{4}{5}$ $\frac{31}{100}$

$2\frac{7}{10}$ $3\frac{17}{50}$ $1\frac{1}{4}$ $\frac{1}{2}$

6 MIXED NUMBERS

$\frac{23}{4}$ $\frac{11}{4}$ $\frac{17}{6}$

$\frac{13}{4}$ $\frac{10}{3}$ $\frac{13}{5}$ $\frac{27}{8}$

$\frac{19}{8}$ $\frac{13}{6}$ $\frac{8}{3}$ $\frac{19}{10}$

$\frac{7}{4}$ $\frac{12}{7}$ $\frac{11}{7}$ $\frac{25}{16}$

7 ADDITION

$\frac{9}{16}$ $\frac{7}{15}$ $\frac{8}{9}$

$\frac{3}{4}$ $\frac{5}{7}$ $1\frac{2}{3}$ $\frac{6}{7}$

$\frac{17}{30}$ 1 $2\frac{1}{3}$ $1\frac{1}{3}$

$\frac{9}{11}$ $1\frac{1}{3}$ $\frac{1}{2}$ $\frac{5}{8}$

8 ADDITION

$7\frac{1}{2}$ $7\frac{4}{7}$ $3\frac{4}{5}$

$9\frac{2}{3}$ $3\frac{1}{2}$ $6\frac{4}{9}$ $6\frac{3}{4}$

$8\frac{4}{5}$ $4\frac{7}{9}$ $7\frac{1}{4}$ $7\frac{3}{4}$

$7\frac{4}{9}$ $6\frac{6}{13}$ $8\frac{3}{5}$ $5\frac{1}{2}$

9 ADDITION

$9\frac{2}{3}$ $5\frac{5}{12}$ $10\frac{3}{10}$

$9\frac{4}{11}$ $6\frac{2}{9}$ $9\frac{5}{7}$ $7\frac{4}{7}$

$5\frac{3}{5}$ $6\frac{2}{9}$ $8\frac{2}{11}$ $13\frac{1}{8}$

$18\frac{1}{10}$ $16\frac{1}{12}$ $10\frac{1}{8}$ $10\frac{5}{6}$

10 ADDITION

$1\frac{6}{7}$ $1\frac{7}{8}$ $4\frac{3}{7}$

$10\frac{1}{8}$ $3\frac{5}{12}$ $2\frac{5}{14}$ $2\frac{2}{15}$

$8\frac{3}{16}$ $2\frac{3}{11}$ $12\frac{2}{11}$ $6\frac{1}{10}$

$9\frac{1}{7}$ $4\frac{5}{6}$ $1\frac{3}{4}$ $4\frac{7}{8}$

11 ADDITION

$8\frac{1}{2}$ 15 $4\frac{2}{3}$

$2\frac{2}{3}$ $7\frac{1}{5}$ $6\frac{1}{4}$ 5

12 $10\frac{1}{3}$ $3\frac{1}{3}$ $4\frac{1}{4}$

$18\frac{1}{4}$ $4\frac{1}{2}$ $20\frac{1}{3}$ $2\frac{1}{4}$

12 REVIEW

$\frac{11}{13}$ $6\frac{2}{3}$ $3\frac{1}{10}$

$1\frac{1}{8}$ $7\frac{1}{5}$ $3\frac{1}{4}$ $4\frac{7}{8}$

$13\frac{3}{5}$ $\frac{2}{3}$ $5\frac{1}{11}$ $8\frac{2}{7}$

$1\frac{1}{7}$ $1\frac{1}{2}$ $\frac{12}{17}$ $8\frac{1}{2}$

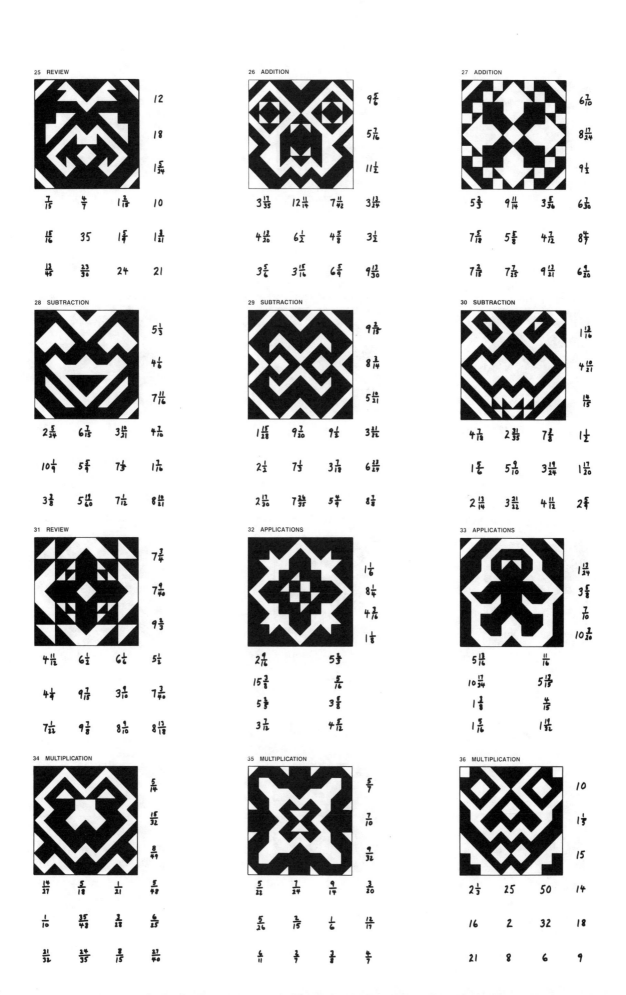

25 REVIEW

12
18
1 5/24

7/15	4/7	1 1/18	10
1 5/16	35	1 5/7	1 8/21
13/45	23/30	24	21

26 ADDITION

9 5/6
5 7/16
11 1/2

3 11/35	12 11/14	7 11/48	3 13/24
4 13/20	6 1/2	4 5/8	3 1/2
3 5/6	3 15/16	6 5/9	9 13/30

27 ADDITION

6 7/10
8 17/24
9 1/2

5 2/3	9 11/14	3 5/36	6 7/30
7 5/18	5 5/8	4 7/12	8 4/7
7 2/13	7 7/25	9 13/21	6 1/20

28 SUBTRACTION

5 1/3
4 1/6
7 11/16

2 5/24	6 7/15	3 10/21	4 7/10
10 1/9	5 5/7	7 1/3	1 7/16
3 3/8	5 11/60	7 1/12	8 13/21

29 SUBTRACTION

9 2/15
8 3/14
5 11/21

1 15/28	9 7/20	9 1/2	3 11/12
2 1/2	7 1/3	3 7/18	6 23/24
2 17/20	7 24/35	5 4/7	8 1/8

30 SUBTRACTION

1 11/16
4 10/21
14/15

4 7/18	2 31/35	7 3/8	1 1/2
1 5/6	5 9/10	3 19/24	1 17/20
2 13/14	3 21/22	4 11/12	2 4/7

31 REVIEW

7 3/4
7 9/40
9 2/3

4 11/12	6 1/2	6 1/6	5 1/2
4 1/7	9 7/15	3 9/10	7 3/40
7 1/22	9 7/8	8 9/10	8 13/18

32 APPLICATIONS

1 1/6
8 1/4
4 7/16
1 1/8

2 9/16	5 3/7
15 3/8	5/16
5 3/7	3 3/8
3 7/12	4 5/12

33 APPLICATIONS

1 13/24
3 5/8
7/10
10 7/20

5 13/16	11/16
10 17/24	5 13/15
1 1/8	4/15
1 5/16	1 11/12

34 MULTIPLICATION

5/14
15/32
8/49

14/27	5/18	1/21	5/48
1/10	35/48	3/18	6/25
21/32	24/35	8/15	27/40

35 MULTIPLICATION

5/7
7/10
9/32

5/22	7/24	9/14	3/20
5/26	3/15	1/6	13/17
6/11	3/7	3/8	4/7

36 MULTIPLICATION

10
1 1/3
15

2 1/3	25	50	14
16	2	32	18
21	8	6	9

37 MULTIPLICATION

54

36

40

$4\frac{2}{3}$	20	35	44
$5\frac{2}{3}$	45	24	66
16	21	30	60

38 MULTIPLICATION

$\frac{1}{2}$

$2\frac{17}{23}$

$1\frac{11}{13}$

$1\frac{4}{5}$	$3\frac{3}{10}$	$4\frac{2}{5}$	$1\frac{5}{16}$
$2\frac{3}{26}$	$1\frac{11}{17}$	$1\frac{9}{10}$	$1\frac{1}{3}$
$2\frac{1}{3}$	$\frac{9}{10}$	$1\frac{10}{11}$	$2\frac{6}{17}$

39 MULTIPLICATION

$5\frac{1}{4}$

$3\frac{1}{2}$

4

8	$2\frac{2}{5}$	18	6
24	$3\frac{1}{5}$	14	32
12	45	$4\frac{4}{5}$	3

40 REVIEW

$\frac{15}{28}$

20

6

$8\frac{1}{4}$	2	12	$11\frac{1}{3}$
$4\frac{1}{2}$	$\frac{1}{2}$	28	$1\frac{1}{6}$
5	25	$\frac{1}{42}$	$2\frac{1}{2}$

41 DIVISION

$\frac{2}{3}$

1

$2\frac{1}{2}$

3	$1\frac{1}{2}$	$1\frac{1}{6}$	$1\frac{1}{11}$
$\frac{5}{6}$	$\frac{3}{4}$	$1\frac{1}{3}$	$2\frac{1}{4}$
2	$\frac{4}{5}$	9	$\frac{1}{3}$

42 DIVISION

27

12

10

33	28	30	35
48	16	90	40
42	36	14	18

43 DIVISION

6

$15\frac{1}{2}$

$12\frac{2}{3}$

$3\frac{1}{2}$	$3\frac{3}{5}$	$1\frac{7}{8}$	14
10	8	24	$7\frac{1}{2}$
$8\frac{3}{4}$	4	5	$5\frac{2}{3}$

44 DIVISION

$1\frac{5}{7}$

$\frac{3}{10}$

6

$\frac{2}{7}$	$\frac{1}{4}$	$3\frac{10}{13}$	$\frac{2}{15}$
$\frac{1}{14}$	$\frac{3}{5}$	$\frac{1}{24}$	$\frac{1}{6}$
$\frac{5}{12}$	24	$\frac{8}{23}$	$1\frac{1}{9}$

45 DIVISION

$1\frac{1}{2}$

$\frac{7}{8}$

$\frac{2}{7}$

$\frac{5}{8}$	$\frac{4}{11}$	$\frac{2}{3}$	$\frac{2}{5}$
$\frac{4}{7}$	$\frac{3}{4}$	$\frac{1}{10}$	$1\frac{1}{3}$
$1\frac{1}{7}$	$\frac{3}{5}$	$\frac{3}{8}$	$\frac{3}{7}$

46 DIVISION

$1\frac{7}{9}$

4

6

$4\frac{4}{5}$	$8\frac{5}{8}$	$\frac{3}{5}$	$1\frac{3}{5}$
$\frac{2}{3}$	$1\frac{5}{7}$	$1\frac{12}{13}$	$2\frac{1}{4}$
$\frac{3}{4}$	$1\frac{1}{2}$	$7\frac{4}{11}$	$2\frac{1}{7}$

47 REVIEW

$1\frac{5}{9}$

10

8

1	$\frac{4}{9}$	5	$\frac{1}{12}$
$5\frac{5}{9}$	4	$\frac{2}{21}$	$1\frac{1}{2}$
6	$1\frac{3}{5}$	$\frac{4}{21}$	$6\frac{2}{5}$

48 APPLICATIONS

$4\frac{2}{3}$

3

$\frac{7}{16}$

195

34	$1\frac{1}{8}$
14	805
4	$11\frac{1}{4}$
$1\frac{7}{8}$	36